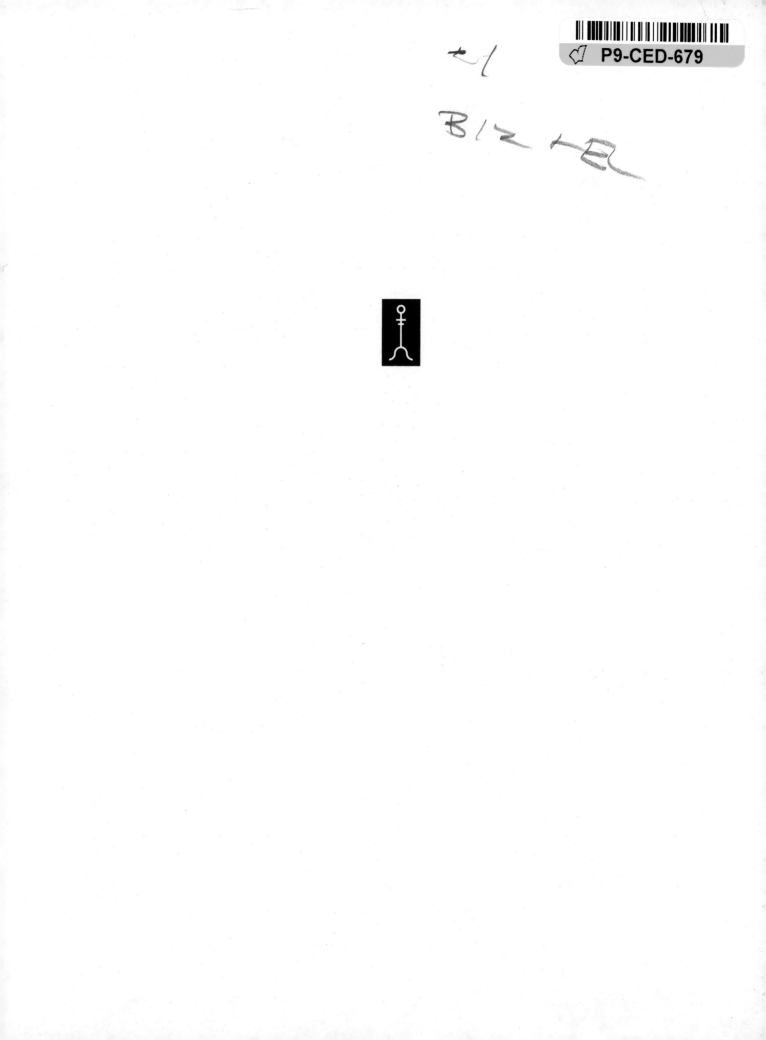

# The Buffettology Workbook

## Value Investing the Warren Buffett Way

MARY BUFFETT AND DAVID CLARK

A FIRESIDE BOOK
Published by Simon & Schuster
New York London Toronto Sydney Singapore

FIRESIDE
Rockefeller Center
1230 Avenue of the Americas
New York, NY 10020

FIRESIDE and colophon are registered trademarks
of Simon & Schuster, Inc.

Designed by Christine Weathersbee

Manufactured in the United States of America

10   9   8   7

Library of Congress Cataloging-in-Publication Data is available.

ISBN-13: 978-0-684-87171-4
ISBN-10:    0-684-87171-8

# DISCLAIMER

This publication contains the opinions and ideas of its authors. It is not a recommendation to purchase or sell the securities of any of the companies or investments herein discussed. It is sold with the understanding that the authors and publisher are not engaged in rendering legal, accounting, investment or other professional services. Laws vary from state to state and federal laws may apply to particular transaction, and if the reader requires expert financial or other assistance or legal advice, a competent professional should be consulted. Neither the authors nor the publisher can guarantee the accuracy of the information contained herein.

The authors and publisher specifically disclaim any responsibility for any liability, loss or risk, professional or otherwise, which is incurred as a consequence, directly or indirectly, of the use and application of any of the contents of this book.

# CONTENTS

INTRODUCTION 9

**PART I:** 15
**UNDERSTANDING VALUE INVESTING**

1: Short-Sightedness and the Bad News Phenomenon: 17
The Gifts that Keep On Giving

2: Identifying the Economic Engine Warren Wants to Own 21

3: Identifying the Sick/Commodity Type Business 25

4: The Healthy Business: The Consumer Monopoly 38
(Where Warren Finds All the Money)

5: Determining if the Business Has a Consumer Monopoly 45

6: Where to Look for a Consumer Monopoly 68

7: The Bad News that Creates a Buying Situation 78

**PART II:** 85
**WARREN BUFFETT'S INTRINSIC VALUE EQUATIONS**

8: Finding the Company and the Numbers 87

9: Financial Calculation #1: Predictability of Earnings 91
at a Glance

10: Financial Calculation #2: A Test to Determine Your 97
Initial Rate of Return

11: Financial Calculation #3: Test for Determining 99
the Per Share Growth Rate

12: Financial Calculation #4: Relative Value to Treasury Bonds 104

13: Financial Calculation #5: Understanding Warren's 107
Preference for Companies That Earn High Rates
of Return on Shareholders' Equity

14: Financial Calculation #6: Determining the Projected Annual 115
Compounding Rate of Return: Part I

15:    Determining the Projected Annual Compounding     122
Rate of Return: Part II

16:    Financial Calculation #7: The Equity/Bond with     130
an Expanding Coupon

17:    Financial Calculation #8: Using the Per Share Earnings     134
Annual Growth Rate to Project an Investment's
Compounding Annual Rate of Return

18:    Financial Calculation #9: Why Warren Loves Stock     138
Repurchase Programs, or, How Can a Company Increase
Its Shareholders' Fortunes By Buying Back the Company's Stock

19:    Financial Calculation #10: How to Determine if Per Share     145
Earnings Are Increasing Because of Share Repurchases

20:    Financial Calculation #11: How to Measure Management's     148
Ability to Utilize Retained Earnings

21:    Financial Calculation #12: The Internet and Warren's     153
Short-Term Arbitrage Commitments

22:    Doing It Yourself: Buffettology Worksheet     161

23:    Bringing It All Together: The Case Studies     169

# INTRODUCTION

The Buffettology Workbook is designed to teach you the investment methodologies of Warren Buffett. Warren has never been the type of investor who "plays" the stock market. In fact, over the last forty years, he has made a point of dodging every popular investment mania to sweep Wall Street. Be it the Internet revolution or the biotech bonanza, he sat out all the big plays, never making, as he himself admits, one thin dime off any of them. Yet, in those years, as countless treasure-laden Wall Street ships slipped by, Warren managed to turn an initial investment of $105,000 into a fortune exceeding $30 billion, solely by investing in the stock market. His investment feat is unparalleled in the history of Wall Street.

How did Warren Buffett become a multibillionaire, King of the Street, without making any money off any of the big Wall Street plays? It's an interesting question.

The answer may not be obvious but it is simple: Warren Buffett got super rich not by playing the stock market (you heard me right, he doesn't *play* the stock market) but by playing the people and institutions that play the stock market. Warren is the ultimate exploiter of the folly that results from other investors' short-sightedness. The people and institutions that play the stock market in search of quick profits will at some point (we can assure you) commit acts of short-sightedness that ultimately collapse into investment foolishness. When they do, Warren is there waiting, patiently, to take advantage of them. It sounds predatory, doesn't it? It is.

Warren is able to do this better than anyone else because he discovered something that very few people appreciate, that approximately 95% of the people and investment institutions that make up the stock market are what he calls "short-term motivated." They respond to short-term stimuli—they buy on good news and sell on bad.

The good news can be as complex as a prospective buyout looming on the horizon or as simple as a quarterly increase in earnings or a quickly rising stock price. The bad news can be anything from a major industry recession to simply missing a quarterly earnings projection by a few cents.

Warren realized that an enthusiastic stock price, when coupled with good news about a company, was often enough to help push the price of a company's shares into the stratosphere. This is commonly referred to as the "good news phenomenon." He also saw that the opposite happened when the situation was reversed. A pessimistic price, when coupled with negative news about a company, will send its stock into a tailspin. This is, of course, the "bad news phenomenon."

Warren discovered that in both situations the underlying long-term economic value of the company's business is often totally ignored. The short-term mentality of the stock market sometimes grossly *overvalues* a company, just as it sometimes grossly *undervalues* a company.

Warren also observed that, over time, it is the *long-term economic value* of a business that levels the playing field and ultimately causes the stock market to properly value the company relative to its long-term worth as a business enterprise. Warren has found that businesses that the stock market has overvalued are eventually revalued downward, making their shareholders poorer. This means that many a fashionable investment ends up in the dumps, costing its shareholders their fortunes, rather than earning them a bonanza. He also discovered that many overlooked and undervalued businesses are eventually revalued upward, making their shareholders richer. Which means a current stock market pariah can often end up tomorrow's shining star.

The aspect of this treasure hunt that intrigues Warren, and where he made the majority of his money, is when the short-term market mentality grossly undervalues a *great* business. He has determined that the stock market will sometimes overreact to bad news about a great business and rush to sell its stock, making it a bargain buy for the few who value the stock based on its predictable long-term economics. (Remember, the vast majority of people and institutions, like mutual fund managers, sell on bad news.) When this happens to a stock that Warren is watching, he goes into market and buys as many shares as he can, knowing that over time, the long-term economics of the business will eventually correct the negative situation and return the stock's price to more profitable ground.

Warren, unlike the vast majority of the market, loves to buy on *bad news*.

He shops when the stocks are unpopular and the prices are cheap—when short-term doom and gloom blinds Wall Street's eyes to the predictable long-term economic value of a great business.

Speculating in good news bull markets is something that Warren leaves to the other guys. It's not his game. He never owned Yahoo!, Lucent Technologies, CMGI, or any of the other high-flying high-tech companies that were all the rage of the Internet bubble. Warren's game is to avoid popular stocks, wait for short-term bad news to drive down the price of some fantastic business, then jump on it with a ton of cash, buying as many shares as he can.

*The Buffettology Workbook* is designed to teach you tools that will give you the kind of conviction that Warren has to charge ahead where others fear to tread. We'll take you step by step through the methodology and financial equations Warren uses, not only to determine *what* companies to invest in, but also *when* to invest in them. Simply knowing what types of companies have excellent long-term economics working in their favor is not enough. You also have to know how to determine the right price to pay for them. Pay too high a price and it doesn't matter how great an economic engine the company has working for you, your investment return is forever moored to the dock of poor results. Pay a low enough price for the right business and you too can sail away with the riches of King Solomon, just as Warren has.

The first part of this book focuses on the qualitative side of the equation. This is where you'll learn how Warren identifies the power and quality of a company's long-term economics. It explains how he determines whether or not the company's economic machinery is sound enough to weather the storm that brought the company's stock price down in the first place. You will come to see that Warren's genius lies in his ability to grasp the long-term economic worth of a handful of great businesses and why they are sometimes oversold by the stock market.

The second part is quantitative. This is where you will learn to use the mathematical equations that Warren uses to determine how much to pay for one of these great businesses. Warren will only invest in a company when it makes business sense, when he can get it at the right price, as determined by projecting an annual compounding rate of return for the investment. This projected annual compounding rate of return is ascertained by performing a series of calculations that we will teach you how to do.

To facilitate the number crunching, we incorporate into the book the use of a Texas Instruments BA-35 Solar financial calculator. Thirty years ago these marvelous little wonders didn't exist, but thanks to the brilliance of Texas Instruments, a world that once belonged only to Wall Street analysts is now accessible and understandable to anyone. So if you are afraid of financial math—don't be; we've got you covered and in no time you'll be making financial projections just like you-know-who. (Please note: Though we have designed the workbook around the use of this particular calculator, any financial calculator that performs present and future value calculations will suffice.)

At the end of the book we have created several case studies and a special template for you to use to facilitate the use of Warren's methodology and intrinsic value equations. This will enable you to work through a set of specific questions and calculations to help you obtain Warren's unique perspective.

Those of you who have read *Buffettology* will find that the Workbook will give you a very different, but enlightening, perspective on Warren Buffett's investment methods. We have revisited many of the original *Buffettology* case studies to determine whether our past analysis was on the money. (It was and still is.) We also explore how Internet trading companies have made stock arbitrage a lucrative venture for even the smallest of individual investors.

For those of you who haven't read *Buffettology,* we can think of no better primer than the Workbook. Each book complements the other; reading both should give you a deeper and more profitable understanding of Warren Buffett's investment techniques. While *Buffettology* focused on Warren's use of Business Perspective Investing, the Workbook takes an in-depth look at just how he uses the stock market's short-term mentality to reap unheard-of riches.

You will learn that this short-term mentality has permeated every corner of the investment world, and that if it didn't exist, Warren would never have made a penny. But it does and he has used it to create one of the great fortunes of all time.

Please don't be misled. Warren's methods are fairly simple to grasp, but they do go against basic human intuition. The learning part is easy. The implementation is far more difficult. This book will be read and understood by many, but few will have the courage to implement its methods. Buying on bad news is much harder than it sounds. The few who come to understand his methods and develop the backbone to implement them will soon discover a bottomless well of wealth into which they may dip for the rest of their lives.

So let's get out the calculator, sharpen a pencil or two, find a clean piece of paper, and start calculating our way to *your first billion!*

---

# KEY POINTS
# FROM THIS CHAPTER

- **Warren is not interested in popular investments such as Internet companies.**

- **Warren discovered that the vast majority of stock market investors are short-term oriented, that they buy on good news and sell on bad.**

- **The short-term stock market mentality sometimes grossly undervalues the long-term prospects of a great business. When it does this, Warren becomes interested.**

- **Warren likes to buy on bad news.**

- **Warren's genius lies in his ability to grasp other people's ignorance about the long-term economic worth of certain businesses.**

---

## Study Questions

Are you more comfortable buying on good or bad news? Why?

Is Warren more interested in buying on good or bad news? Why?

Why do you think that most investors ignore the long term and focus on the short term?

Have you ever wished you had the courage to invest in a company after the market tanked its stock? What was the company's name and how much money would you have made if you had bought and held?

## True or False

1. T or F     Warren is interested in buying Internet stocks that are grossly overvalued.

2. T or F     The time Warren becomes interested in a company is when it has just announced

good news about the business and the price of its shares responds by jumping upward.

3.  T or F    The stock market sometimes undervalues a company from a long-term perspective.

4.  T or F    Even great businesses can fall prey to the "bad news phenomenon."

Answers: 1. False 2. False 3. True 4. True

# PART ONE

# Understanding Value Investing

# 1: SHORT-SIGHTEDNESS AND THE BAD NEWS PHENOMENON: THE GIFTS THAT KEEP ON GIVING

Short-sightedness and the bad news phenomenon. What are these things and what do they have to do with Warren Buffett? The answer is everything.

If the vast majority of the stock market were not short-sighted, Warren Buffett would never have an opportunity to buy some of the world's greatest businesses at discount prices. He could never have bought 1.7 million shares of *The Washington Post* twenty-seven years ago for approximately $6.14 a share. *The Washington Post* now trades at approximately $500 a share, which makes his $10.2 million initial investment worth approximately $863.8 million today. That equates to a pretax annual compounding rate of return of 17.8%. Without the short-sightedness of the stock market, Warren could not have bought Coca-Cola for $5.22 a share twelve years ago. It now trades at approximately $50 a share, which equates to a pretax *annual* compounding rate of return of approximately 21%.

Warren discovered early on in his career that 95% of the participants in the stock market, from Internet day traders to mutual fund managers who manage billions, are only interested in making a quick buck. Yes, some pay lip service to the importance of long-term investing, but in truth they are stuck on making fast money.

Warren found that no matter how intelligent a person is, the nature of the beast controls the investor's actions. Take mutual fund managers. If you talk to any of them, they will tell you that they are under great pressure to produce the highest yearly results possible. This is because mutual funds are marketed to a lay public that is only interested in investing in funds that earn top performance ratings in any given year. Imagine a mutual fund manager telling his or her marketing team that their fund ranked in the bottom 10% for performance out of all the mutual funds in America. Do you think the marketing team would jump up and down with joy and go out and drop a couple of million on advertising to let the world know that their fund ranked in the bottom 10%? No. More likely our underperforming fund manager would lose his or her job and some promising young hot shot would take over the fund's investment allocations.

Don't believe it? Ask people you know why they chose to invest in a particular mutual fund and they will more than likely tell you it was because the fund was ranked as a top performer. The nature of the mutual fund beast influences a lot of very smart people into playing a short-term game with enormous amounts of capital. No matter what fund managers' personal convictions may be, producing the best short-term results possible is the way to keep their job.

Warren also discovered that investors who get caught up playing a short-term game have very human reactions whenever they hear bad news about a company in which they own shares—they sell them. To make the big bucks in the short-term game, the investor has to be one of the first to get in on the stock before it moves up, and one of first to get out before it moves down. Having access to the most up-to-date information available is of utmost importance. A good earnings report and the stock price moves upward. A bad earnings report and it moves downward. It doesn't matter whether earnings will improve in a year or two. All that anybody is interested in is what is going to happen today. If things look great this week, people will buy the stock, and if they look bad next week, they will sell it. This is why mutual funds are notorious for having such high rates of investment turnover. They get in and out of a lot of different stocks in hopes of beating the other guys in the competition for the all-important title Top Fund of the Year.

This "bad news phenomenon"—the selling of shares on bad news—is one constant in the ever-changing world of stock market trading. Watch any nightly business report on television and you'll see that after any negative news about a company is announced, the price of its shares drops. If the news is really bad, the shares will drop like a rock. It's the nature of the beast.

Bad news means falling share prices; bad news means that Warren's eyes light up. To Warren, the short-sightedness of the stock market, when combined with the bad news phenomenon, is the gift that keeps on giving. This combination of factors has produced for him one great buying opportunity after another, year after year, decade after decade, to the happy tune of $30 billion.

Before we jump to the next chapter, we'll let you in on one of Warren's best-kept secrets. He figured out that some, but not all, companies have economic engines that are so powerful they can pull themselves out of almost any kind of bad news mud that the short-sightedness of the stock market gets them stuck in. He has developed a specific list of criteria to help him identify those businesses. When these businesses are hit with bad news and the short-sighted stock market hammers their stock prices, he steps in and buys like crazy. He calls these wonderfully resilient businesses "consumer monopolies." Warren made all his big money by investing in consumer monopolies. They are the Holy Grail of his investment philosophy and we predict that they will be the next great love of your investment life as well.

---

## KEY POINTS
## FROM THIS CHAPTER

- **Warren discovered that everyone from mutual fund managers to Internet day traders are stuck playing the short-term game. It is the nature of the stock market.**
- **The bad news phenomenon is a constant—people sell on bad news.**
- **Companies that have consumer monopolies have the economic power to pull themselves out of most bad news situations.**
- **Warren made all his big money investing in consumer monopolies.**

---

## Study Questions

Why are most mutual funds fixated on short-term results?

How does Warren use a long-term perspective to exploit the stock market's short sightedness?

## True or False Questions

1. T or F    Mutual fund managers are short-term motivated because they market their products to an investment public that is extremely short-sighted.

2. T or F    The majority of the investing public sells on bad news and buys on good.

3. T or F    Warren buys on bad news.

4. T or F    Consumer monopolies have the strong economic engines.

Answers: 1. True 2. True 3. True 4. True

# 2: IDENTIFYING THE ECONOMIC ENGINE WARREN WANTS TO OWN

**W**hat are the characteristics of the businesses that Warren Buffett wants to invest in? After more than forty-five years of actively investing in common stocks, Warren has discovered that if you want to take advantage of the stock market's short-sightedness, coupled with the bad news phenomenon, you must invest in companies with economics that will let them survive and prosper beyond the negative news that created the original buying situation.

Remember, Warren is an exploiter of the investors and mutual funds that sell their shares on bad news. To do this he has to make sure that the company he is investing in is not only an intrinsically sound enterprise, but also has the economic ability to excel and earn fantastic profits. Warren isn't only interested in bottom picking. He's interested in using the market's mistakes to become the owner of some of America's greatest business enterprises at bargain prices. *By picking only the cream of the crop, he is able to ensure that over a period of time the share price will not only fully recover, but will continue its upward trajectory.* It is nothing for Warren to see a dramatic increase in the value of one of these great business after he buys in. In the case of Geico he saw a 5,230% increase in value. And with *The Washington Post* he did even better, clocking in with a 7,930% increase in value. It's mind-blowing, isn't it? He bought into these companies at a time when all of Wall Street was running from them as if they had the plague. He held on to them, because they were fantastic businesses that had the kind of economics working in their favor that over time would make him tremendously wealthy.

Think of it this way. You have two racehorses. One, called Healthy, has a great track record with lots of wins. The other, Sickly, has a less than average track record. Both manage to catch the flu and are out of action for a year. The value on both shrinks because neither is going to win any money this racing season. So their owners, intending to cut their losses, offer them up for sale. Which would you want to invest your money in? Healthy or Sickly?

It's not hard to see that Healthy is the best bet. First of all, you know that Healthy is fundamentally a strong horse. Not only does Healthy have a better chance of recovering from the flu than Sickly does, but afterward Healthy will be winning lots of races and make you tons of money!

Even if Sickly recovers, the horse will more than likely remain true to its name and get sick again and again. The return on your investment will be like Sickly's health—poor.

Warren has separated the world of business into two different categories. The first one is the sickly kind; these are companies that have poor economics working in their favor. *He refers to these as "commodity" type businesses.* A commodity type of business manufactures or sells a generic product that a lot of other businesses also make or sell. The second type of business is the healthy kind, which has terrific business economics working in its favor. Think of Coca-Cola, Geico, and *The Washington Post.* He calls these companies *"consumer monopolies." A consumer monopoly is the kind of business that sells a brand name product or has a unique position in the stream of commerce that allows it to act like a monopoly.* Thus, if you want that particular product or to use a company's specific service, *you have to purchase it from that company and no one else.* This gives the company the freedom to raise prices and have higher earnings. These companies also have the greatest potential for long-term economic growth. They experience fewer ups and downs in business and they possess the wherewithal to weather the storms that a short-sighted stock market invariably overreacts to.

First things first. Warren believes that unless you can identify these two different types of businesses, you will be unable to exploit the pricing mistakes of a short-sighted stock market. You have to know what a commodity type business is and be able to identify its characteristics. If you don't, you just may end up owning one. You also have to be able to identify what a consumer monopoly type business is and be able to identify its characteristics, because this is the type of business that will make you a pot of gold.

Let's take a deeper look into both these kinds of businesses, so you will be able to determine which is which, and which one is going to make you rich. As Warren says: "A stock well bought never has to be sold."

# KEY POINTS
# FROM THIS CHAPTER

- Warren has separated the world of business into two different categories: the healthy consumer monopoly type business and the sick commodity type business.

- A consumer monopoly is a type of business that sells a brand name product or has a unique position that allows it to act like a monopoly.

- A commodity type business is the kind that manufactures a generic product or service that a lot of companies produce and sell.

- Warren believes that if you can't identify these two different types of businesses, you will be unable to exploit the pricing mistakes of a short-sighted stock market.

## Study Questions

Why has Warren divided the world of business into two categories?

Can you think of a company that has a consumer monopoly?

Can you think of a company that sells a commodity type of product?

## True or False

1.  T or F    Warren is interested in buying the sick commodity type of business.

2.  T or F    Warren is interested in buying the healthy consumer monopoly type business.

3.  T or F    A commodity type of business is the kind that manufactures a brand name product.

4.  T or F     A consumer monopoly type of business is
              the kind that manufactures a generic type
              of product.

# 3: IDENTIFYING THE SICK/COMMODITY TYPE BUSINESS

**W**arren identifies the sick kind of business as a "commodity type business." The commodity type business is a company that sells a generic type of product or service in which price is the single most important motivating factor in the consumer's decision to buy. Some of the most simple and obvious commodity type businesses that we deal with in our daily lives are:

- airlines
- producers of raw foodstuffs (such as corn and rice)
- steel producers
- gas and oil companies
- the lumber industry
- paper manufacturers
- automobile manufacturers

All of these companies sell a commodity for which there is considerable competition in the marketplace. The business that offers the lowest price is most likely to get our money. Thus, the price of the product becomes the single most important motivating factor for the consumer in making a buy decision.

People buy gasoline on the basis of price, not on the basis of brand loyalty, even though the oil companies would like us to believe that one brand is better than the other. The lower-priced gasoline wins the day. The same goes for such goods as concrete, lumber, bricks, memory and processing chips for your computer (although Intel is trying to develop brand name recognition for its processing chips). Automobile manufacturers are also selling a commodity type product, for within each segment of the auto market, manufacturers compete to sell the product with the most bells and whistles at the lowest possible price. Airlines are notorious for pricing wars. The airline with the lowest-priced seats attracts the most business.

Let's face it. It really doesn't matter where the corn you buy comes from. Nor does it really matter which airline you are flying from Los Angeles to San Francisco on, as long as it gets you there. GM and Ford both manufacture and sell nearly identical trucks, but if the Ford truck is a lot cheaper, and you will probably buy the Ford. This intense level of price competition leads to very low profit margins.

*In commodity type businesses the low-cost producer wins. This is because the low-cost provider has larger profit margins, which gives it more freedom to set prices at levels that drive out the competition.* Costs are lower. Therefore, profit margins are potentially higher. It's a simple concept but it has complicated implications. In order to be the low-cost producer in most cases, the company must constantly make manufacturing improvements that will keep the business competitive. This requires additional capital expenditures, which tend to eat up earnings, which might otherwise have been spent on new product development or acquiring new enterprises—expenditures that would have increased the underlying value of the company.

The scenario usually works like this: Company A makes improvements in its manufacturing process, which lowers its cost of production, which increases its profit margins. Company A then lowers the price of its product in an attempt to take a greater market share from Companies B, C, and D.

Companies B, C, and D start to lose business to Company A and respond by making the same improvements to their manufacturing processes as Company A. Companies B, C, and D then lower their prices to compete with company A and in the process destroy any increase in A's profit margin that the original improvements created. And then the vicious cycle repeats itself.

Occasionally these kinds of businesses do well. In a boom economy, in which consumers' desire to spend outstrips the available supply, producers like auto manufacturers earn a bundle. Responding to meet the increase in demand, they take their bloated balance sheet and expand their operations—a decision that will cost them billions. Their shareholders, seeing all the new wealth, will want their cut and the company consents to their demands by raising the dividend payout. The unions, seeing how well the company is doing, will stick their hands out as well. The company pays them too. Then when the boom period is over—and all booms do eventually end—they will be stuck with excess production capacity, a fat quarterly dividend payout, and a very expensive union workforce that isn't going away. Suddenly, their fat balance sheet starts to bleed real money. Consider this: Between 1990 and 1993, during a mild recession, General Motors bled $9.6 billion. In a serious recession auto manufacturers bleed even more and the $20 billion or so that they have socked away for a rainy day suddenly doesn't look like much of a cushion. The next thing you know they are shutting down plants and cutting dividends, which means the stock price tanks. It's not a pretty sight.

Other more specific events have boosted these companies' incomes. When Hurricane Hugo smashed into Florida and destroyed thousands of homes, the cost of sheet plywood shot through the roof. Anyone in the plywood business in Florida that year did very well. During the summer, when huge numbers of people travel, the airlines really sock it in. Occasionally an auto manufacturer hits a home run with a hot new vehicle that customers have to have, like Chrysler's minivan. At times like these, all the producers and sellers make substantial profits. But any increase in demand is usually met with an increase in supply. Then when demand slackens, the excess supply drives prices and profit margins down again.

Additionally, a commodity type business is entirely dependent upon the quality and intelligence of management to create a profitable enterprise. If management lacks foresight or wastes the company's precious assets by allocating resources unwisely, the business could lose its position as the low-cost producer, thus opening itself up to competitive attack and possible financial ruin.

From an investment standpoint, the commodity type business is the kind Warren avoids. First, these companies' profits are kept low because of price competition, so the money just isn't there to expand the business or to invest in new and more profitable business ventures. Second, even if they do manage to make money, this capital is usually spent upgrading plant and equipment to keep abreast of the competition. In some businesses, standing still for a moment offers your competitors all the opportunity that they need to destroy you. Many of these companies carry the added weight of huge long-term debts. In 1999 GM carried approximately $55 billion in long-term debt, a sum considerably greater than the $34 billion it made from 1990 to 1999. GM could take every dollar they made in the last ten years and still would not have enough to pay off their long-term debt. Ford, GM's rival, managed over the last ten years to earn a total of approximately $35.1 billion against a long-term debt burden in 1999 of approximately $70 billion. If Ford continues with its historic financial performance, it will take the company approximately twenty years to pay off its long-term debt. Doesn't sound like a great business, does it? Imagine that you own a company that carries this sort of long-term debt and suddenly the boom is over. Guess who is going to lose a ton of cash? That long-term debt becomes a long-term noose.

The airlines really aren't any different. In 1999, United Airlines, one of the best-run airlines in the world, carried a long-term debt burden of approximately $5 billion against $4 billion in total net income for the last ten years. TWA has lost money every year for the last five years. Unions and high fixed costs ensure that any airline flying the friendly skies will never allow their shareholders' riches to soar for very long.

Commodity type businesses sometimes try to create product distinction by bombarding consumers with advertising touting their product as superior to the competition's. In some instances considerable product modifications move one company ahead of the pack—for a while, anyway. The problem, however, is that no matter what enhancements a commodity type business makes, consumers are ultimately motivated by price alone; the company that is the low-cost producer will be the winner and the others will end up struggling.

Warren loves to use Burlington Industries, a manufacture of textiles, a commodity type product, to illustrate this point. In 1964 Burlington had sales of $1.2 billion and the stock sold for an adjusted-for-splits price of around $30 a share. Between 1964 and 1985 the company made capital expenditures of about $3 billion, or about $100 a share, on improvements to become more efficient and therefore more profitable. The majority of the capital expenditures were for cost improvements and expansion of operations. Although the company reported sales of $2.8 billion in 1985, it had lost sales volume in inflation-adjusted dollars. It was also getting far lower returns on sales and equity than it did in 1964. The stock in 1985 sold for $34 a share, or a little better than it did in 1964. Twenty-one years of business operations and $3 billion in shareholder money spent, and still the stock had given its shareholders only a modest appreciation.

The managers at Burlington are some of the most able in the textile industry. It's the industry that has the problem. Poor economics, which developed from excess competition, resulted in a substantial production overcapacity for the entire textile industry. Substantial overcapacity means price competition, which means lower profit margins, which means lower profits, which means a poor performing stock and disappointed shareholders.

Investing in Burlington in a market downturn or on bad news would position an investor in a situation that might not work out and has little or no potential for long-term growth. It is the kind of investment that Warren steers away from because it is not the kind of investment that will make him or anyone else rich.

Warren is fond of saying that when management with an excellent reputation meets a business with a poor reputation it is usually the business's reputation that remains intact. Which means that no matter who is running the show, there is no possible way of turning a company with inherently poor business economics into one with excellent business economics. Ugly ducklings only grow up to be beautiful swans in fairy tales. In the business world they stay ugly ducklings no matter which managerial prince kisses them.

## IDENTIFYING THE SICK COMMODITY TYPE BUSINESS

Identifying a commodity type business is not that difficult; they usually are selling something that a lot of other businesses are selling. Characteristics include low profit margins, low returns on shareholders' equity (shareholders' equity is defined as a company's total assets *less the company's total liabilities*), difficulty with brand name loyalty, presence of multiple producers, substantial excess production capacity in the industry, erratic profits, and profitability that is almost entirely dependent upon management's abilities to efficiently utilize tangible assets like plant and equipment.

The basic characteristics of a commodity business are:

- **Low profit margins on sales coupled with low inventory turnover.** Slow inventory turnover when coupled with low profit margins produces lousy returns on capital. This means that the company doesn't make any money.

  The ideal business situation is high profit margins and high inventory turnover (high profit margins with lots of sales mean lots of money). Businesses with slow inventory turnover can be highly profitable—if the profit margins are extraordinary. (We don't sell much, but the profit margins on what we sell are incredible!) You can also have low profit margins as long as you have high inventory turnover. (Our profit margins stink, but we make up for this by selling a ton of these things!) The classic example of this is Berkshire Hathaway's Nebraska Furniture Mart, which has lousy margins because it sells everything so cheap, but makes up for it with incredible inventory turnover (it sells a ton of stuff). Customers are elated with low prices and its owners make lots of money.

  Think of it this way. Say you have a lemonade stand in the desert and the lemonade costs you $1 a glass to make. If you can sell it for a million dollars a glass you don't need to turn over your inventory many times to get rich. Sell one glass and you have it made. This is a case of low inventory turnover, with fantastic profit margins. You'll also make a ton of money if you charge $2 and you can sell 20 million glasses a year. Either way you end up rich.

If you are looking at a company that has low profit margins, it is more than likely a commodity type business—the type that will always be plagued with problems and low profits.

Go to *The Value Line Investment Survey,* Yahoo! Finance, MSN.com, or another provider of financial information that lists businesses' net profit margins. (*Value Line* is the investment source that Warren prefers. It's a paid for service that follows more than 1,600 different companies and is the source of all the financial figures used in this book.) Now find the net profit margins for the following five companies in their respective industries:

1. Burlington Inds.—Textiles ___%
2. Coca-Cola—Beverage ___%
3. UAL Corp.—Airline ___%
4. Microsoft—Software ___%
5. Boise Cascade—Paper ___%

Just based on what is in front of you, which of the above companies would you rather own an interest in?_____Which company would you least want to own?_____

My own check of *Value Line* provided the following net profit margin values:

1. Burlington Inds.—Textiles 1.4%
2. Coca-Cola—Beverage 16.3%
3. UAL Corp.—Airline 4.4%
4. Microsoft—Software 38.6%
5. Boise Cascade—Paper 2.2%

As of this writing, *Microsoft* is clearly the most profitable and *Burlington Industries* the least profitable.

- **Low returns on shareholders' equity.** Low returns on shareholders' equity are a good indication that the company you are looking at is a commodity type. Since the average return on shareholders' equity for an American corporation is 12%, anything below that may indicate the presence of poor business economics created by commodity type products and pricing. Warren believes that without high returns on shareholders' equity it is impossible for a company to truly prosper over the long run. We will discuss this concept later on in greater detail, but for now, what we are looking for are high returns on shareholders' equity. (Again, both *Value Line* and MSN.com list the return on shareholders' equity for thousands of different companies.)

Low returns on shareholders' equity are what we want to stay away from. Find the 1999 rate of return on equity for the following five companies:

1. Burlington Inds.—Textiles     ___%
2. Coca-Cola—Beverage     ___%
3. UAL Corp.—Airline     ___%
4. Microsoft—Software     ___%
5. Boise Cascade—Paper     ___%

Answer:

1. Burlington Inds.—Textiles     3.6%
2. Coca-Cola—Beverage     32.5%
3. UAL Corp.—Airline     15.5%
4. Microsoft—Software     26.8%
5. Boise Cascade—Paper     10%

- **Absence of any brand name loyalty.** If the brand name of the product you just bought doesn't mean a lot, you can bet you are dealing with a commodity type business. Retailers that sell commodity type products sometimes can create a brand name with their store—a reputation for good service and fair prices may keep bringing customers back. But stores like this can't make a buck unless they have high inventory turnover, so they need lots of sales to make up for the rotten profit margins attached to selling commodity type products.

List five companies that sell a product that has an absence of brand name loyalty (we give you the first one):

1. <u>Boise Cascade—Paper</u>

2. _____

3. _____

4. _____

5. _____

- **Presence of multiple producers.** Go into any auto supply store and you will find seven or eight different brands of motor oil, all of them selling for about the same price. Want to catch a plane from NYC to Los Angeles? Seven or eight airlines are going to compete for your business. If you want to buy a new SUV, you have five or six auto manufacturers to choose from.

  Multiple producers breed competition and competition breeds lower prices. Lower prices breed lower profit margins, and lower profit margins mean lower earnings for shareholders. List five companies that sell products where there are multiple producers selling the same or similar product.

1. <u>UAL Corp.—Airline</u>

2. _____

3. _____

4. _____

5. _____

- **Organized labor.** When the low-cost producer wins, organized labor has enormous power to damage a business, which it can leverage to demand a higher cut of the company's profit. This is especially true whenever you find heavy investment in capital equipment, accompanied by high fixed costs. When airplane pilots strike, they can cripple an airline. Suddenly the airline is hemorrhaging money, because a fleet of airplanes is enormously expensive to own and maintain even if none of them are flying. As soon as the auto manufacturers start showing an increase in profits, the labor unions demand higher salaries for their auto workers. In situations like these, unions become demanding quasi-owners with whom shareholders must constantly share their wealth or risk a strike that could lead to the financial ruin. List five companies that have to use organized labor:

1. <u>Ford Motor</u>
2. _____
3. _____
4. _____
5. _____

- **Existence of substantial excess production capacity in the industry.** An industry with substantial excess production capacity can't really profit from an increase in demand until the excess production capacity is used up. Then and only then can prices start to rise. However, when prices rise, management is invariably consumed with the urge to grow. Grand visions of huge industrial empires dance in their heads. And with pockets full of shareholders' riches derived from the increase in demand and prices, management will set forth on the ultimate folly. They will expand production and in the process create even *more* production capacity.

The problem is that the guys down the street, the competition, have the same idea. Soon everybody expands production and we are back at square one—an industry riddled with overcapacity. Overcapacity means price wars and price wars mean lower profit margins and profits. And then everything starts all over again.

To check for excess capacity, find out if product prices have been rising or declining over the last five to ten years. Make sure you factor in inflation when you make your calculation. If prices have been declining, it's a good indication that the industry may be suffering from excess capacity.

List five companies that might suffer from excess production capacity:

1. <u>Boise Cascade—paper</u>
2. _____
3. _____
4. _____
5. _____

- **Erratic Profits.** Wildly erratic profits are a good indication that you are dealing with a commodity type business. A survey of a company's net earnings for the last ten years will usually show any boom or bust patterns that are endemic to the commodity type business. A good place to check to see if a company suffers from erratic profits is *Value Line,* Yahoo! Finance, or MSN.com.

  If yearly per share earnings of the business in question look like this—

  | Year | Earnings |
  |------|----------|
  | 1990 | $1.57 |
  | 1991 | $(1.16) loss |
  | 1992 | $(0.28) loss |
  | 1993 | $0.42 |
  | 1994 | $(0.23) loss |
  | 1995 | $0.60 |
  | 1996 | $1.90 |
  | 1997 | $2.39 |
  | 1998 | $0.43 |
  | 1999 | $(1.69) loss |

  —then you might suspect that it is a commodity type business.

  List five companies that suffer from erratic profits:

  1. General Motors
  2. _____
  3. _____
  4. _____
  5. _____

- **Profitability is almost entirely dependent upon management's abilities to efficiently utilize tangible assets.** Anytime profitability of a company is largely dependent upon the business's ability to efficiently utilize its tangible assets, such as plant and equipment, and *not* on identifiable assets such as *patents, copyrights,* and *brand names,* you should suspect that the company in question is of the commodity type. An airline must keep hundreds of millions of dollars in jet aircraft not only flying, but filled with paying passengers. The airline's ability to make money comes from its ability to utilize its jet aircraft, its tangible assets. The same can be said of automobile manufacturers with their billion-dollar plants. Their ability to utilize their enormous investment in tangible assets has a tremendous impact on their ability to make money.

List five companies where profitability is almost entirely dependent upon management's abilities to efficiently utilize tangible assets.

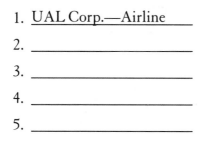

    1. <u>UAL Corp.—Airline</u>

    2. _____

    3. _____

    4. _____

    5. _____

## SUMMARY

Remember, if price is the single most important motivating factor when purchasing a product, then you are most likely looking at a commodity type business. At best, the company will present you with only average results over the long term and will have great difficulty recovering from any type of misfortune. These businesses present their management teams with one difficult decision after another and they will present their shareholders with one disappointing year after another.

If you are like Warren and are in the business of exploiting the stock market's short-sightedness, coupled with the bad news phenomenon, then the commodity type businesses are the ones to avoid. They get sick easily and have a hard time recovering. When they do get well, they don't stay well for very long.

---

# KEY POINTS FROM THIS CHAPTER

- Commodity type businesses have the following characteristics:
  - Low profit margins on sales coupled with low inventory turnover
  - Low returns on shareholders' equity
  - Absence of any brand loyalty
  - Presence of multiple producers
  - Existence of substantial excess production capacity in the industry
  - Erratic profits
  - Profitability that is almost entirely dependent upon management's abilities to efficiently utilize tangible assets.

---

## Study Questions

Why do low profit margins, when combined with low inventory turnover, result in poor profitability?

Can you name a company that has erratic profits and sells a commodity type product?

Why are commodity type businesses the ones to stay away from if you are exploiting the stock market's short-sightedness?

## True or False

1. T or F    Low returns on shareholders' equity are characteristic of commodity type businesses.

2. T or F    A commodity type product usually only has a single manufacturer.

3.  T or F    Commodity type businesses don't usually have erratic profits.

4.  T or F    When exploiting the stock market's short-sightedness, commodity type businesses are the ones to stay away from.

Answers: 1. True 2. False 3. False 4. True

# 4: THE HEALTHY BUSINESS: THE CONSUMER MONOPOLY (WHERE WARREN FINDS ALL THE MONEY)

Warren is only interested in companies that are healthy long-term and have great economics working in their favor. He calls these consumer monopolies. Warren discovered that these companies hold a kind of monopoly on the products or services they sell. This allows them to earn the fantastic profits that result from monopoly pricing.

Warren often uses the toll bridge analogy to explain the concept of the consumer monopoly. If you, the consumer, want to cross a river without swimming or riding in a boat, you have to cross on a bridge. To use the bridge you have to pay the toll. The toll bridge has a kind of monopoly on river crossing at that particular place.

Think about it. If you want to chew a piece of Wrigley's gum, you have to buy it from the Wm. Wrigley Jr. Company, a business that Warren has long coveted. The same can be said of a large town with only *one* newspaper. If you want to advertise in the paper, you have to pay the advertising rate the paper is charging or you can't advertise in the local paper. These companies have a monopoly on what consumers want, thus giving these businesses freedom to charge higher prices—which mean higher profit margins, which mean greater profits for the shareholders.

Consumer monopolies, though incredible businesses, are still subject to the ups and downs of business cycles and the occasional business calamity (New Coke, anyone?) As such, their stock prices can fall prey to the market's short-sightedness. Bad news will send stock prices downward, even for these types of companies, creating a potential buying situation. But Warren knows that the underlying excellent economics that these businesses possess will act like a kind of lifesaver that will eventually pull them out of any troubled water into which they fall. It is a scenario that Warren has watched over and over again with such companies as Geico, American Express, Coca-Cola, *The Washington Post,* Capital Cities, and Freddie Mac.

In this chapter we'll address how to identify the exceptional business that has a consumer monopoly working in its favor. What does Warren Buffett want to buy? Inherently healthy companies that have consumer monopolies and have suffered a decline in the price of their stock due to the market's short-sightedness.

## WARREN IS SEARCHING FOR A COMPANY WITH A CONSUMER MONOPOLY

To get the mental juices flowing, let's take a quick jaunt back in time and look at some early thinkers who addressed the investment value of the consumer monopoly.

In 1938, an enterprising student at Johns Hopkins University, by the name of Lawrence N. Bloomberg, wrote his doctoral dissertation on the investment value of the consumer monopoly. His dissertation, entitled *The Investment Value of Goodwill,* compared the investment values of companies that had consumer monopolies to companies that were commodity type businesses. Bloomberg thought that consumer goodwill created what Warren calls the consumer monopoly. Bloomberg wrote that although goodwill is a state of mind, it adheres to the company because of *distinctive attributes that are particularly attractive to buyers who then form an attachment to a company and the products it sells.*

Bloomberg thought that consumer goodwill could be associated with a business that has a convenient location, courteous employees, prompt deliveries, and satisfactory products. He also thought that persistent and alluring advertising would keep a particular product or trade name in the buyers' minds when they make their purchase. Or maybe, through the possession of a secret process or patent, a company is able to supply an unusual or slightly different product—like the secret process for making Coca-Cola or Microsoft's patent for the Windows operating system.

Bloomberg believed that with the above factors working in a company's favor, it could obtain superior results, which he equated with higher returns on shareholder's equity, superior earnings growth, and improved performance of the stock. He also discovered that the shares of these companies would outperform the rest of the market whether the economy expanded or contracted.

Warren has developed a conceptual test to determine the presence of such a consumer monopoly. In testing for the presence of a consumer monopoly, he asks himself the following questions:

1. If the company in question paid out as a dividend its entire net worth, so that it had a zero shareholders' equity, would there still be any value to the company? If the answer is yes, then there is a good chance that the company owns a consumer monopoly. Warren used this rationale when he made his original investments in Geico and American Express. Both of these companies had suffered business calamities that had destroyed their balance sheets, essentially reducing their net worth to zero. But American Express, with its American Express card, and Geico, being a low-cost producer, still possessed the consumer monopolies that were the fountain of their original wealth. Warren invested in them and made a killing on both.

2. If he had access to billions of dollars (which he does), and his pick of the top fifty managers in the country (which he also has), could he start a business and successfully compete with the business in question? If the answer is a resounding no, then the company in question is protected by some kind of strong consumer monopoly. He used this rationale when he made his original investments in Coca-Cola and Gillette, two companies that have obtained close to world dominance in their industries.

You should mark in your notebooks that in Warren's world the real test of the strength of a consumer monopoly is how much damage a competitor could do even if he didn't care about making money. Is it possible to compete with *The Wall Street Journal?* You could spend billions and still not put a dent in its readership. Could you start a chewing gum company and compete with Wrigley's? Several have tried and several have failed. How about that Hershey's chocolate bar? Or Coca-Cola?

Driving in the high mountains of Indonesia a few years ago, I pulled over to a roadside stand to get something to drink. At this small stand in the middle of nowhere, in a country with almost no signs of Americana, there was only one brand of soda for sale, Coca-Cola.

Think about Coca-Cola for a moment. Every gas station, movie theater, supermarket, restaurant, fast food joint, Kwik Shop, bar, hotel, and sporting arena sells Coca-Cola. In every office building in America you can bet that somewhere there is a vending machine stocked with Coca-Cola waiting to take your money. Coca-Cola is such a popular drink that stores and restaurants have to carry it. THEY HAVE TO CARRY IT! They have to carry it because if they don't they will lose sales. Can you name one other brand name product that every one of these vendors has to carry?

To compete with Coca-Cola you would need the capital base of two General Motors, and you would probably still fail. Talk about a consumer monopoly! I personally have consumed thousands of servings of the beverage. How about you? Your children?

What about Marlboro cigarettes? Ever try to convince a Marlboro smoker to switch brands? And how many people use Gillette razors every morning? Do you think that you could get them to change? What about Microsoft's Windows operating system. Could you convince someone to give it up in favor of another system? What about all those McDonald's hamburgers we've eaten over the last forty years?

My personal test for a consumer monopoly is to ask this question: If someone gave me the rights to a particular brand name like Marlboro or Wrigley, or the rights to the name and secret formula of Coca-Cola, would the investment bankers at Merrill Lynch or Goldman Sachs consent to raise the billions I would need to start production? If the answer is yes, I know it's time to start pouring the champagne.

If you were the owner of the only water company in town, you could make a ton of money. The only catch is that the populace long ago had the common sense to regulate the water industry. The same can be said for electric companies. Great businesses, but regulations keep the owners from obtaining superior results. What you want is an unregulated water or electric company.

The problem is that when the investment community recognizes them, their stock prices rise astronomically. Since the price you pay determines the rate of return, paying a steep price means a smaller rate of return. So the trick is finding a water company that the rest of the world has yet to identify or to make your investment in a consumer monopoly when the short-sighted stock market has overreacted to some bad news.

Bloomberg thought that one of the reasons companies with strong consumer monopolies were so profitable was that they did not have to rely heavily on investments in land, plant, and equipment. Such fixed charges and property taxes loom large in the cost of production of their counterparts (the commodity type businesses).

In contrast, the wealth of companies with consumer monopolies is principally in the form of intangible assets, such as the secret formula to Coca-Cola or the brand name Marlboro. Inasmuch as federal taxation is practically confined to earnings, the taxes paid by these companies tend to vary with profits, while the taxes paid by companies with heavy investments in physical assets, like General Motors, are not so flexible. Beyond the very early stages of expansion, the physical asset/commodity type business can only meet the increasing demand for its products by incurring heavy costs for plant expansion.

Companies that benefit from *consumer monopolies,* because of their large cash flows, are often nearly debt free. Companies like Wm. Wrigley Jr. (maker of chewing gum) and UST Inc. (maker of chewing tobacco) have little or no debt on their balance sheets. This gives them a great deal of freedom to pursue other profitable ventures or purchase back their own shares. Additionally, they're often manufacturers of low-tech products that don't require sophisticated manufacturing plants. Also, since there is little competition biting at their heels, their manufacturing facilities are long-lived. They are free of the costs of having to constantly retool and build new plants to keep up with competitors.

General Motors, manufacturer of a price-sensitive commodity type product, has to spend billions of dollars to retool and build new production facilities to get a new model car to market. It's a product that may stay competitive for only a few years before GM has to go back to the drawing board and build again. Companies like Wm. Wrigley Jr. and Hershey Foods, on the other hand, have probably been using the same equipment for the last fifty years. Gum and chocolate just aren't high-tech items and the machinery for making them probably wears out before it becomes obsolete.

It is worth noting that the history of commerce indicates that various forms of the consumer monopolies phenomenon have existed since the beginning of trade. From the Venetians, who profited greatly off their monopoly on the trade of high-quality textiles from the Far East, to the British Empire's early consumer monopoly on high-quality steel, to the early American West, where the names Colt and Winchester meant quality firearms, to Germany's famed cannon maker, Krupp, whose products were found on both sides of the two world wars—all of these businesses profited from the consumer's perception that their product quality and services were unique and worth paying for.

Think of General Electric, the company that Thomas Edison helped start, and the profits it made electrifying the planet. GE sold a country the know-how to make electricity and the products to wire it, and then they sold the populace electric appliances, lightbulbs, power tools, and refrigerators. (Kind of like Gillette giving away the razor in order to get the customer to buy the razor blades.) To this day GE is one of America's most powerful commercial enterprises. A power derived in part from the huge amount of capital it acquired in the early part of this century when it was the only game in town.

Today, Microsoft has a virtual monopoly with its Windows computer operating system. Microsoft has fantastic profit margins and amazing returns on shareholders' equity. It is a veritable money machine and has made its shareholders outrageously wealthy. Warren and Bill Gates have both learned that the consumer monopoly is the ticket to extraordinary wealth!

## KEY POINTS FROM THIS CHAPTER

- **A consumer monopoly is a type of toll bridge business. If you want to buy a certain product you have to purchase it from that one company and no one else.**

- **Warren's test for a consumer monopoly is to ask himself whether it would be possible to create a competing business even if one didn't care about losing money.**

- **A consumer monopoly sells a product where quality and uniqueness are the most important factors in the consumer's decision to buy.**

- **Consumer monopolies, though excellent businesses, are still subject to the ups and downs of the business cycle and the occasional business calamity.**

## Study Questions

Why does the consumer monopoly act like a lifesaver when the company suffers a business setback?

Can you think of why a company's intangible assets, like a brand name or patent, might be far more valuable than its tangible assets?

If you could earn all the profits from the sale of a particular product currently being produced today, which one would it be? Why?

List ten companies that you think sell brand name consumer monopoly type products:

1.     <u>Gillette—razors</u>

2.     _____

3.     _____

4.     _____

5.     _____

6.     _____

7.     _____

8.     _____

9.     _____

10.    _____

## True or False

1.  T or F     A toll bridge is a type of consumer monopoly.

2.  T or F     A consumer monopoly has the ability to recover from almost any business setback.

3.  T or F     To a consumer monopoly type business a brand name can be far more valuable than the company's tangible assets.

4.  T or F     Consumer monopolies are immune to the ups and downs to the business cycle.

Answers: 1. True 2. True 3. True 4. False

# 5: DETERMINING IF THE BUSINESS HAS A CONSUMER MONOPOLY

If you're looking for buried treasure, you'd better have a good idea where it's hidden before you start digging. Warren has discovered certain identifiable characteristics that help determine whether a business in question has a consumer monopoly, and whether it's resilient enough to weather the vicissitudes of a short-sighted stock market.

We have found that it is easier to break this part of the analysis into a series of questions. Warren uses a similar line of questioning when he is trying to identify a consumer monopoly and determine how strong the business's long-term economics are.

First, let's walk through the questions:

## No. 1:

*Can You Identify a Consumer Monopoly Type Product or
Service that the Company Sells?*

## No. 2:

*Do Historical Earnings Show a Strong and Upward Trend?*

## No. 3:

*Is the Company Loaded with Debt?*

## No. 4:

*Does the Company Earn a High Rate of Return
on Shareholders' Equity?*

### No. 5:

*Does the Company Have to Spend a High Percentage of Its Retained Earnings to Maintain Its Current Operations?*

### No. 6:

*Are Retained Earnings Free to be Invested in New Businesses or Used to Repurchase the Company's Shares?*

### No. 7:

*Is the Company Free to Adjust Prices for Inflation?*

### No. 8:

*Will the Value Added by Retaining Earnings Lead to an Increase in the Stock Market Value of the Company?*

These eight questions will help guide you through the dark forest of investment babble. It's kind of like trying to figure out whether your blind date is a hopeful for the altar. Ever been married? Been to college? Have a good job? Snore?

We do the same thing when we allocate capital to investment. As Warren says, in the field of investing it is better that one act as a Catholic and marry for life. That way one makes sure going in that the partner chosen is one worth keeping—because there is no getting out.

Let's look at these questions in detail.

## NO. 1

### Can You Identify a Consumer Monopoly Type Product or Service that the Company Sells?

Is there a consumer monopoly here? It's the first question you have to ask. You're looking for a brand name product or a key service that people or businesses are dependent on. Products are much easier to identify than services, so let's start with them.

Go stand outside a convenience store, supermarket, pharmacy, bar, gas station, or bookstore, and ask yourself *what are the brand name products that this business has to carry to be in business?* What products would a manager be insane not to carry? Make a list.

Now go inside and examine the product. If it's got a brand name that you immediately recognize, then the chances are good that there is some kind of consumer monopoly at work.

Name a newspaper you can buy at any newsstand in America—*USA Today*. Name a soda that you can buy anywhere in the world—Coca-Cola. Name a brand of cigarette that every convenience shop carries—Marlboro. Who owns the rights to *The Little Mermaid* movie that your children can't seem to get enough of? Disney. What kind of breakfast cereal is your child eating? What kind of razor blades do you use every morning? Take a walk around the local supermarket and go wild.

Companies that provide *services* that constitute consumer monopolies are much harder to identify. Key places to look are in the field of advertising—television networks and advertising agencies; and key financial service providers—such as credit card companies. (Don't worry. The chapter just ahead tells you exactly where to look for companies that have consumer monopolies.)

Just because the business has a brand name product working in its favor does not mean that it is an excellent business. Management could fail to maximize the magic of a consumer monopoly in any number of ways.

So after you zero in on one you must begin a quantitative/qualitative process of analysis of the company and its management. A great product or service is where you start, but a great product or service doesn't necessarily have a great company behind it.

List ten brand name products that you use in your everyday life and the companies that manufacture them.

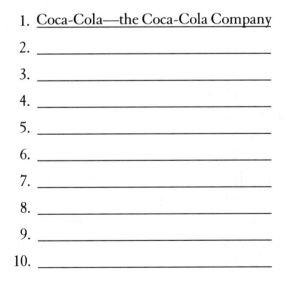

1. Coca-Cola—the Coca-Cola Company
2. _____
3. _____
4. _____
5. _____
6. _____
7. _____
8. _____
9. _____
10. _____

## NO. 2

## Do Historical Earnings Show a Strong and Upward Trend?

A consumer monopoly is a great thing, but management may have done such a poor job running the rest of the company that annual per share earnings fluctuate wildly. Warren is looking for annual per share earnings that are strong and show an upward trend. (Again, *Value Line,* Yahoo! Finance, or MSN.com can supply you with the earnings histories of thousands of companies.)

Does the per share earnings picture for the company in question look like Company I or Company II?

| COMPANY I | | COMPANY II | |
|---|---|---|---|
| **Year** | **Per Share Earnings** | **Year** | **Per Share Earnings** |
| 1990 | $1.07 | 1990 | $(1.57) loss |
| 1991 | $1.16 | 1991 | $0.06 |
| 1992 | $1.28 | 1992 | $0.28 |
| 1993 | $1.42 | 1993 | $0.42 |
| 1994 | $1.64 | 1994 | $(0.23) loss |
| 1995 | $1.60 | 1995 | $0.60 |
| 1996 | $1.90 | 1996 | $(1.90) loss |
| 1997 | $2.39 | 1997 | $2.39 |
| 1998 | $2.43 | 1998 | $(1.25) loss |
| 1999 | $2.69 | 1999 | $0.99 |

Warren would be interested in Company I and not Company II. Company II's per share earnings have been way too erratic to predict with any certainty. Regardless of any competitive advantage Company II's products may have, there's something going on behind those earnings gyrations. We might suspect that it is, in fact, a commodity type business. Warren would not consider Company II a buying opportunity.

Company I shows a per share earnings picture that may indicate not only a company that possesses a consumer monopoly product or products, but also a company whose management can turn that advantage into real shareholder value.

The really big consumer monopoly buying opportunities are going to happen either when the entire stock market suffers a setback, as was the case when Warren started buying *The Washington Post* and Coca-Cola, or when the company experiences a business setback that depresses its current earnings, as was the case when Warren bought Geico and his first purchase of American Express.

Stock market downturns and panics are easy to spot and understand, but a calamity that causes a reduction in a company's net earnings must be throughly understood before you invest. It may be that an entire industry is suffering from a cyclical business recession or it could be that a company has a single division that is giving it problems. **Warren believes that a wonderful investment opportunity exists when a company suffers a onetime solvable problem that the stock market has overreacted to.**

When a business with a consumer monopoly suffers a setback, the per share earnings might look like Company III or Company IV.

## COMPANY III

| Year | Per Share Earnings |
|------|--------------------|
| 1990 | $1.07 |
| 1991 | $1.16 |
| 1992 | $1.28 |
| 1993 | $1.42 |
| 1994 | $1.64 |
| 1995 | $1.60 |
| 1996 | $1.90 |
| 1997 | $2.39 |
| 1998 | $2.43 |
| 1999 | $(1.22) → Shows an actual loss |

## COMPANY IV

| Year | Per Share Earnings |
|------|--------------------|
| 1990 | $1.07 |
| 1991 | $1.16 |
| 1992 | $1.28 |
| 1993 | $1.42 |
| 1994 | $1.64 |
| 1995 | $1.70 |
| 1996 | $1.90 |
| 1997 | $2.39 |
| 1998 | $1.75 |
| 1999 | $0.52 → Shows a sharp decline |

Company III has an excellent history of long-term earnings growth, but shows a sudden earnings loss. This kind of thing is immediately suspect and should be thoroughly investigated to determine the nature of the loss. Is it an anomaly or a sign of things to come? Is it something that can be corrected?

Company IV, on the other hand, has a strong earnings history, but shows a troubling earnings decline in 1998 and 1999 with no real loss. This too is a suspect situation, but it shouldn't be written off. A thorough investigation might reveal that it has a huge potential for long-term profit, the kind that Warren is always interested in. Warren says that this type of investment idea should hit you over the head. The stock market is like a stream in which you occasionally find hunks of gold so huge that you'd have to be blind to miss them.

List ten companies that have historical per share earnings that are strong and show an upward trend:

1. Microsoft _____
2. _____
3. _____
4. _____
5. _____
6. _____
7. _____
8. _____
9. _____
10. _____

List ten companies that have historical per share earnings that are strong and show an upward trend but were having problems in 1999:

1. Coca-Cola _____
2. _____
3. _____
4. _____
5. _____
6. _____
7. _____
8. _____
9. _____
10. _____

## NO. 3

### Is the Company Loaded with Debt?

Warren wants his potential investment candidates to be conservatively financed. If a company has a great consumer monopoly, then more than likely it is spinning off tons of cash and is in no need of a long-term debt burden. (*Value Line,* MSN.com, and Yahoo! Financial all list the long-term debt figures for thousands of companies.)

Warren has found that traditional methods of ascertaining the financial strength of a company, such as the debt to shareholders' equity ratio, are poor indicators of the financial power of a business. This is because a company's assets are never a source of funds to service or retire debt unless the company is being liquidated. Banks loan money to businesses on their ability to service the debt, and any shareholders' equity in the company is merely additional safety. Warren has found that most capital equipment is so unique to the business that it is worthless to anyone else, even though it might be carried on the books at considerable value. Warren has discovered that the wealth of a company's assets, tangible and intangible, is in its ability to produce wealth via earnings.

The best test, then, of a company's financial power is in its ability to service and pay off debt out of its net earnings. Consumer monopolies, like Warren's favorites Wrigley's, UST, and International Flavor & Fragrances, often have little or no long-term debt. Warren's star performer, Coca-Cola, carries a long-term debt burden of less than one year's current net earnings. Think about it. The earnings for a single year can wipe Coke's balance sheet squeaky clean. In 1999, Gannett Co. had $990 million in net earnings and $1 billion in long-term debt, so it would take Gannett a little better than one year's net earnings to pay off all of its long-term debt. The same year Gillette had net earnings of $1.2 billion and long-term debt of $2.4 billion, so it would take approximately two years of net earnings to pay off its long-term debt.

In contrast, a commodity type business like GM in 1999 carried approximately $55 billion in long-term debt, a sum considerably greater than its total net earnings of approximately $34 billion for the ten-year period from 1990 to 1999. As we said earlier, if you took every dollar that GM earned in the last 10 years, you still couldn't pay off its all its long-term debt. Ford Motor Company isn't in any better shape. Over the last ten years it managed to earn a total of approximately $35.1 billion against a long-term debt burden in 1999 of approximately $70 billion.

With a consumer monopoly, there is usually lots of money in the bank and little or no debt. In other words, the company has substantial financial firepower to solve almost any problem that the business might suffer. A company that has a lot of debt and no cash reserves may not have the financial power to get itself out of trouble, which is certainly not good for the stock and might even mean a total loss for investors.

Sometimes an excellent business with a consumer monopoly will add a large amount of debt to finance the acquisition of another business. This happened when Capital Cities more than doubled its long-term debt burden to acquire the ABC television and radio networks. In a case like this you have to figure out whether the acquisition is also a consumer monopoly, as ABC was. If it isn't, watch out!

When long-term debt is used to acquire another company, the rule is:

- When two consumer monopolies go to the altar, it will more than likely be a fantastic marriage. With two consumer monopolies spinning off a lot of excess cash, it doesn't take long to reduce mountains of debt to molehills. You can buy into a situation like this on bad news and expect the financial wealth of the two consumer monopolies to turn the situation around.

- When a consumer monopoly marries a commodity type business, the result is usually mediocre. This is because the commodity type business will eat up the profits of the consumer monopoly business to support its poor economics, leaving little to pay down the newly acquired debt. The exception is when the management of a commodity type company uses the company's cash flow to acquire a consumer monopoly type business, and then after the marriage, jettisons the cash-hungry commodity type business. Exploiting this bad news situation entails a great deal more risk and should only be undertaken after careful analysis. When in doubt, Warren likes to sit patiently and wait for the right pitch. You should too.

- When a commodity type business marries another commodity type business, the result is usually a disaster. Neither can produce sufficient profits to climb out of debt. Taking advantage of a bad news/short-sighted market situation in this case usually means disaster to your pocketbook.

To determine whether you can take advantage of a bad news situation, look at whether the company has a consumer monopoly and is conservatively financed. Warren discovered that this type of healthy business is the best and safest bet when playing on the stock market's short-sightedness.

List ten companies that have total long-term debt of less than three times current net earnings:

1. Coca-Cola _____

2. _____

3. _____

4. _____

5. _____

6. _____

7. _____

8. _____

9. _____

10. _____

## NO. 4

### Does the Company Earn a High Rate of Return on Shareholders' Equity?

Warren has figured out that high returns on shareholders' equity can produce great wealth for shareholders. Thus, Warren seeks to invest in companies that **consistently** earn high returns on shareholders' equity.

To fully understand why Warren is so interested in high returns on shareholders' equity, let us work through a hypothetical scenario.

Shareholders' equity is defined as a company's total assets less the company's total liabilities. Kind of like the equity in your house. Let's say that you bought a house as a rental property and you paid $200,000 for it. To close the deal you invested $50,000 of your own money and borrowed $150,000 from a bank. The $50,000 you invested in the house is your equity in the property.

When you rent out your house, the amount of money that you earn from the rent, after paying your expenses, mortgage, and taxes would be your return on equity. If you rented your house out for $15,000 a year and had $10,000 in total expenditures, then you would be earning $5,000 a year on your $50,000 in equity. The return on your $50,000 in equity would be the $5,000 you earned. This equates to a 10% return on equity ($5, ÷ $50,000 = 10%).

Likewise, if you owned stock in a business (Company A), that had $10 million in assets and $4 million in liabilities, the business would have shareholders' equity of $6 million. If the company earned, after taxes, $1,980,000, we could calculate the business's return on shareholders' equity to be 33% ($1,980,000 ÷ $6,000,000 = 33%).

This means that the $6 million of shareholders' equity is earning a 33% rate of return.

The average return on shareholders' equity for an American corporation over the last forty years has been approximately 12%. This means that, as a whole, year after year, American business earns only 12% on its shareholders' equity base.

Anything above 12% is *above* average. Anything below 12% is *below* average. *And below average is not what we are looking for.*

What Warren is looking for in a business is consistently higher than average returns on shareholders' equity. We are not talking about 12% or 13%, but a rate of return of 15% and above—the higher the better.

Let's look at some of the companies that have caught Warren's interest in the past and see what kind of return on shareholders' equity they got.

The General Foods Corporation was averaging an annual 16% return on shareholders' equity during the time Warren was buying it. Coca-Cola's return on shareholders' equity the year Warren started buying was approximately 33%, and it had had a 25% average annual return on shareholders' equity for the preceding five years. Hershey Foods has long fascinated Warren. Over the last ten years it has had an average annual return on shareholders' equity of 16.7%. Capital Cities had a return on shareholders' equity of 18% when Warren took his position (which he swapped in 1995 for a billion dollars in cash and a big chunk of the ownership of Mickey Mouse—the Walt Disney Company). When Warren started Service Masters, its return on shareholders' equity was in excess of 40%, UST's in excess of 30%, Gannett Co. had a return on shareholders' equity of 25%, and McDonald's was 18%. Warren sees a high return on shareholders' equity as a good indication of the earnings power of a company.

Warren believes that a consistently high return on shareholders' equity is a good indication that the company's management not only can make money from the existing business, but can also profitably employ retained earnings to make more money for the shareholders.

Consistently high returns on shareholders' equity means 15% or better year after year. Warren is not after a company that occasionally has high returns, but one that consistently has high returns.

### Analyzing the Company's Return on Shareholders' Equity

Does the *return on equity picture* of your company in question look like that of Company I or Company II?

| COMPANY I | | COMPANY II | |
|---|---|---|---|
| Year | Return on Shareholders' Equity | Year | Return on Shareholders' Equity |
| 1990 | 28.4% | 1990 | 5.7% |
| 1991 | 31.2% | 1991 | 1.6% |
| 1992 | 34.2% | 1992 | 2.8% |
| 1993 | 35.9% | 1993 | 4.2% |
| 1994 | 36.6% | 1994 | 2.3% |
| 1995 | 48.8% | 1995 | 7.0% |
| 1996 | 47.7% | 1996 | 9.4% |
| 1997 | 48.8% | 1997 | 9.3% |
| 1998 | 55.4% | 1998 | 4.3% |
| 1999 | 56.0% | 1999 | 6.9% |

Warren would be interested in Company I and not Company II. Company II's return on shareholders' equity is way too low. Company I shows a very high rate of return on shareholders' equity that indicates that it benefits from having a very strong consumer monopoly.

There is a great deal more to understanding why Warren is only interested in companies that earn high returns on shareholders' equity, and we go into great detail on this subject in the second part of the book. But for now, remember that Warren is only interested in companies that **consistently** earn a high rate of return on shareholders' equity and that such returns are indicative of the presence of a consumer monopoly.

List ten companies that consistently earn a high rate of return on shareholders' equity.

1. <u>Wrigley—gum</u>
2. _____
3. _____
4. _____
5. _____
6. _____
7. _____
8. _____
9. _____
10. _____

## NO. 5

### Does the Company Have to Spend a High Percentage of Its Retained Earnings to Maintain Its Current Operations?

In the 1934 edition of *Security Analysis,* the late Benjamin Graham, the dean of Wall Street and Warren's teacher and mentor for more than twenty years, introduces his readers to Edgar Lawrence Smith, who in 1924 wrote a book on investing entitled *Common Stocks as Long-Term Investments* (Macmillan). Smith put forth the idea that common stocks should in theory grow in value as long as they earn more than they pay out in dividends, with the retained earnings adding to the company's net worth. In a representative case, a business would earn a 12% return on shareholders' equity, pay out 8% in dividends, and retain 4%. If it did this every year, the stock value should increase with its shareholders' equity, at a rate of 4% compounded annually.

With this in mind, Smith explains the growth of common stock values as arising from the accumulation of asset values through the reinvestment of surplus earnings. Graham, however, warns us that not all companies can reinvest their surplus earnings in expansion of their business enterprises. Most, in fact, must spend their retained earnings on maintaining the status quo; that is, refurbishing expiring plants and equipment. Graham warns the investor that although Smith's fundamental premise is correct—retained earnings will add to the underlying value of a company—more often than not retained earnings are spent just maintaining the status quo, and that they really don't add any real value to a company's underlying net worth.

Warren concluded that Graham's assessment of Smith's analysis was correct for a great majority of businesses. However, he found that under close analysis the consumer monopoly was an exception to the rule. He discovered that over a long period of time, consumer monopolies were able to profitably employ retained earnings at rates of return considerably above the average. In short, Warren found that consumer monopolies usually didn't need to spend their retained earnings upgrading plant and equipment or on new product development, but could spend their earnings on either acquiring new businesses or expanding the operations of their already profitable core enterprises. (These are the kinds of businesses that Warren wants to invest in, because their unencumbered retained earnings not only give them the economic power to easily overcome any business calamity that they might face, but also allow them to grow their shareholders' wealth over the long-term.)

As we said, *making money is one thing, retaining it is another, and not having to spend it on maintaining current operations is still another.* Warren found that in order for Smith's theory to work, he had to invest in companies that 1) made money; 2) could retain it; and 3) didn't have to spend all of their retained earnings on maintaining current operations.

Warren discovered that the capital requirements of the nonconsumer monopoly type business may be so demanding that the company often ends up having little or no money left to increase the fortunes of its shareholders.

Let's look at an example. If a business makes $1 million a year, and retains every cent, but every other year has to spend $2 million replacing plant and equipment that were expended in production, the company really isn't making any money at all. Over the two-year period it's making $2 million and spending the same $2 million—which means that the business is just breaking even. The perfect business for Warren would be one that earns $2 million and spends zero on replacing plant and equipment.

Warren used to teach a night class on investing at the University of Nebraska at Omaha business school. He lectured on the capital requirements of a company and the effect it had on shareholder fortunes. He illustrated this by showing students the past operating records of AT&T and Thomson Publishing.

First Warren demonstrated that before it was broken up, AT&T was a poor investment for shareholders. Although it made a lot of money, it was regulated and it had to plow even more money than it made into capital requirements—research and development and infrastructure. The way that AT&T financed the expansion was to issue more shares and to sell a lot of debt.

On the other hand, Thomson Publishing, which owned a bunch of newspapers in one-newspaper towns, made a lot of money for its shareholders. Once a newspaper builds its printing infrastructure it has little in the way of capital needs to suck away the shareholders' money. In Thomson's case there was a lot of cash to spend on buying more newspapers, thereby making its shareholders richer.

The lesson here is that one business grew in value without requiring more infusions of capital, and the other business grew only because of the additional capital that was invested in it. Imagine that a company that needs constant infusions of capital suffers a business setback. A minor problem may well blossom into a real financial headache because of a general lack of capital. But a business that is spewing out a ton of cash will have no problem financing its way out of almost any difficulty.

Warren is always looking for a consumer monopoly type business that seldom requires replacement of plant and equipment and doesn't require ongoing and expensive research and development. He wants to own a company that produces a product that never becomes obsolete, is simple to produce, and has little or no competition. The only newspaper in town, a candy bar manufacturer, a chewing gum company, a razor blade producer, a soda pop business, a brewery—these are the kinds of companies he loves. Basic businesses that make products that people never want to see change. Predictable product, predictable profits.

List ten companies that don't have to spend the majority of their retained earnings on replacing plant and equipment:

   1. <u>Hershey Foods</u>

   2. _____

   3. _____

   4. _____

   5. _____

   6. _____

7. _____

8. _____

9. _____

10. _____

# NO. 6

## Are Retained Earnings Free to be Invested in New Businesses or Used to Repurchase the Company's Shares?

Another of Warren's keys to defining a great business is that the company must have the capacity to take retained earnings and reinvest them in business ventures that will give them additional high returns.

Think of it this way. If we were to give you $10,000 a year for ten years and you were to put that money your dresser drawer, at the end of ten years you would have saved $100,000.

If you put that $10,000 into a savings account that paid 5% compounded annually, at the end of ten years you would have $132,067.

Let's say that you have Warren's magic touch and could reinvest earnings at a rate of return of 23% compounded annually. At the end of ten years you would have $370,388. That's a couple of hundred thousand dollars more than either the $100,000 in the dresser drawer or the $132,067 in the bank account.

If you were to continue earning a 23% rate of return for a period of twenty years, the wonders of compounding interest would take hold and grow your money to the sum of $3,306,059. That's infinitely greater than the $200,000 you would have had if you had squirreled your money away in the dresser drawer for twenty years. It's also greater than the $347,193 you would have earned if you'd kept hauling those $10,000 payments for twenty years down to the local bank that was paying you 5%.

Warren believes that if a company can employ its retained earnings at above average rates of return, then it is better to keep those earnings in the business. He has stated many times that he is not at all unhappy when Berkshire's wholly-owned businesses retain all of their earnings, as long as they can utilize those funds internally at above average rates of return.

Warren has taken this philosophy and applied it to companies in which he has a minority interest. He believes that if the company has a history of using its retained earnings profitably, earning a rate of return that is above average, it would be to the shareholders' advantage to have the company retain all its earnings. Whether a company pays out a dividend or retains 100% of its earnings is up to the company's board of directors, which means that it doesn't always happen, but when it does it puts a big grin on Warren's face.

Be aware that if a company has low capital requirements but no prospects for capital employment with a high rate of return, or if the management has a history of investing retained earnings into unprofitable projects, *then* Warren believes that the most attractive option for capital employment would be to either pay out the earnings via dividends or use them to repurchase shares.

When retained earnings are used to buy back shares, the company is in effect buying its own property and increasing future per share earnings of the stockholders who didn't sell. If you have a partnership, for instance, and there are three partners, you each in effect own one-third of the business. If the partnership, using partnership funds, buys one of the partners out, then the two remaining partners would each own 50% of the company and split the partnership's future earnings fifty-fifty. Share repurchases will cause per share earnings to increase, which results in an increase in the market price of the stock, which means richer shareholders.

Warren has been a big advocate of share buybacks in all the companies with which he is actively involved. It is a way for him to increase his ownership interest in such companies as Geico, *The Washington Post,* and Coca-Cola without investing another penny. If fact, he has increased his net worth by billions of dollars using this technique. (Chapter 19 gives a detailed explanation of the economics that motivate share repurchase programs.)

Warren sees consumer monopolies as a kind of cash cow. They are very profitable businesses that require very little in further research and development or replacement of plant and equipment. The best cash cows have the ability to invest in or acquire other cash cows. Take RJR and Philip Morris. For years, both companies owned cigarette businesses that were cash cows and generated lots of retained earnings. If they had decided to reinvest those earnings in, say, the automotive business, they could have expected large expenditures for a long time before generating a profit from the operations. They chose instead to take their tobacco-generated earnings and acquire cash cow food companies like Nabisco Foods, General Foods, Kraft Foods, and a myriad other brand name food purveyors. Today, the fantastic wealth-generating machines of these two companies—which used to make their shareholders outrageously wealthy—are being used to pay off a $246 billion settlement with the state governments over tobacco-related illnesses. This is a perfect example of a consumer monopoly using its great financial wealth to bail itself out of trouble. In the case of Philip Morris, if its strategy works, the current stock price of $19 a share may look like the bargain of the new millennium. In case you're wondering, Warren owned RJR and Philip Morris in the '70s and early

'80s, but has shunned them as of late. He likes investing in a sure thing, and neither one comes close to that today.

Another good example of a company that uses this strategy is Sara Lee Corporation. It not only makes brand name cheesecake but has managed to build a portfolio of other consumer brand names such as L'eggs, Hanes, and Playtex.

Capital Cities, before it merged with Disney, used its cash cow cable TV business to buy the ABC television network, another cash cow. For a long time, acquiring other media properties was how it spent most of its money. At one time TV and radio stations were fantastic cash cows. Build a TV station and it lasts for forty years. Until recently, the TV consumer monopoly was protected from competition by the federal government. However, recent expansion of cable, satellite, and interactive TV through the use of telephone lines calls into question whether or not the big three networks—ABC, CBS, and NBC—can protect their business from all the new competition.

Buffett family lore has it that former Capital Cities CEO Tom Murphy was sitting around Warren's home in Omaha, watching TV, when someone remarked, "Isn't it amazing that so many advances have been made in the field of broadcast technology?" Tom said that he liked it better in the old days of black-and-white TV when three networks competed for the advertiser's dollar. Warren believes that the networks may not be the fantastic businesses they once were, but that they are still great businesses.

Determining whether or not company management can utilize its retained earnings is probably the single most important question that you can ask yourself as a long-term investor. Committing capital to a company that has neither the opportunity nor the managerial talent to grow its retained earnings will leave your investment boat dead in the water.

(Once Warren buys a consumer monopoly at a depressed price, he likes to tuck it away in his portfolio and leave it there, watching its retained earnings grow and accumulate, and grow and accumulate, making him richer and richer. A little later on in the book we'll fully explore this compounding effect Warren uses so brilliantly.)

List ten companies that are profitable and have used their retained earnings either to buy new businesses or to repurchase their own shares:

1. Sara Lee _____

2. _____

3. _____

4. _____

5.  _____

6.  _____

7.  _____

8.  _____

9.  _____

10. _____

## NO. 7

### Is the Company Free to Adjust Prices for Inflation?

Inflation means rising prices. The problem with commodity type businesses is that as prices for labor and raw material increase, overproduction may create a situation in which the company has to drop the prices of its products in order to stimulate demand. In this situation, the cost of production is sometimes in excess of the price the product will fetch in the marketplace. This means that the commodity type business will lose a lot of money. This usually results in the company cutting back production, until the excess supply dries up. But that takes time. The laws of supply and demand work, but not overnight. In the meantime, the losses pile up and viability of the business diminishes. (Ranchers are constantly faced with this dilemma. The price of live cattle is dropping, but the costs of feed, fuel, labor, insurance, veterinarians, and grazing land continue to increase. Miscalculate next fall's cattle price and the family ranch may end up in foreclosure.)

This situation occurs periodically in the airline business. Airlines commit themselves to all kinds of heavy fixed costs. Airplanes, fuel, union contracts for pilots, ground crews, mechanics, attendants—all cost a lot of money and all these costs increase with inflation. Then along comes a price war. Suddenly they have to start cutting ticket prices to stay competitive. Want to fly from New York to Los Angeles? A half dozen or more airlines will compete for your business. If one drops prices significantly, they all end up losing. In the 1960s a round trip airplane ticket from Omaha to Paris cost a thousand or more dollars. Recently, you could get one on United for $439 (with air miles). Despite the fact that the cost of airplanes, fuel, pilots, ground crews, mechanics, and those terrible airline meals have more than quadrupled in the last thirty years, my ticket, thanks to a price war, got cheaper. The airline that sold it to me sure didn't get any richer. Now you know why airlines sometimes miss the runway and land in bankruptcy court.

With a commodity type business it is possible to have the cost of production increase along with inflation, while the prices they can charge for their products decrease because of intense competition. Which is not a good situation to be in.

## The Consumer Monopoly and Inflation

For Warren, a business with a consumer monopoly is one that is free to increase the prices of its products right along with inflation, without experiencing a decline in demand. That way its profits remain fat, no matter how inflated the economy gets. A can of Coca-Cola, a Hershey bar, a pack of Wrigley's gum, a six-pack of Budweiser, a carton of Marlboros, have all increased their prices with inflation without experiencing a decline in demand. Yet, the most interesting aspect of the consumer monopoly and inflation is that this increase in product price has also caused an increase in earnings, which has led to an increase in the underlying value of these businesses. Let me explain.

Say that every year, like clockwork, Hershey's sells 10 million chocolate bars. In 1980 it cost Hershey's 20 cents to manufacture each chocolate bar, which was then sold for 40 cents. This gives Hershey's a 20 cent profit on each chocolate bar. To calculate what Hershey's earned selling chocolate bars in 1980, all you have to do is multiply the number sold, 10 million, by the 20 cent profit that each bar produced, which equals $2 million (10 million × $0.20 = $2 million).

So in 1980, Hershey Foods made $2 million selling chocolate bars. If Hershey's has 4 million shares outstanding in 1980, then you could calculate that Hershey's had earnings of $0.50 a share ($2 million ÷ 4 million = $0.50). If Hershey's stock was trading at multiples of 15 in 1980, it would have been trading at $7.50 a share (15 × $0.50 = $7.50).

Jump ahead to 2000; when everything has doubled in price since 1980 because of inflation. Hershey's chocolate bars now cost 40 cents apiece to manufacture and are being sold for 80 cents each. This equates to a profit of 40 cents per chocolate bar. If Hershey's sells 10 million chocolate bars in 2000 (the same number of chocolate bars it sold in 1980) we can calculate that Hershey's will earn $4 million in 2000 or double what it earned in 1980.

(Now comes the really interesting part.) If Hershey's still has 4 million shares outstanding in 2000, the same amount that it had in 1980, it will post a profit of $1 a share ($4 million ÷ 4 million = $1). So in 2000 Hershey's sells the same number of chocolate bars it did in 1980, yet it earns $1.00 a share or $0.50 more than it did in 1980. If you multiply the Hershey's per share earnings of $1.00 by 15, the price to earnings ratio that it had in 1980, you come up with stock price of $15 a share, or $7.50 more than you paid for it back in 1980. The price of a Hershey's chocolate bar doubled and so did the price of your stock.

Hershey's didn't have to manufacture any more chocolate bars in 2000 than it did in 1980. It didn't have to hire any more employees, nor did it have to increase the size of its manufacturing plant. All it had to do was raise prices to stay level with the costs of inflation. As it raised prices, it caused a corresponding rise in the company's stock price.

Don't get all excited and start thinking inflation is a great wealth-building tool. It's not. If prices double, you need to double the amount of money you have just to maintain the purchasing power you started with. What the company with the consumer monopoly offers you is an investment vehicle that will increase in value right along with inflation.

With a **commodity type** business, it is possible to have increasing costs with declining prices, which can spell disaster for the company's stock. With a **consumer monopoly,** however, you have a business that can increase the prices of its products right along with any increases in its costs of production, which means that the underlying value of the company and its stock price will keep up with inflation. What Warren has discovered is that a consumer monopoly type of business is basically inflation proof.

Though actual historical pricing information is hard to obtain, you still should have an idea of what things used to cost years ago. If you are younger and weren't around thirty years ago, ask someone who was. Just to get you started—thirty years ago a Coke cost 10 cents, a Hershey candy bar 5 cents, and a McDonald's hamburger 15 cents. List ten companies that are free to adjust the prices of their products with inflation:

1. <u>Hershey Foods</u>

2. _____

3. _____

4. _____

5. _____

6. _____

7. _____

8. _____

9. _____

10. _____

## NO. 8

### Will the Value Added by Retaining Earnings Lead to an Increase in the Stock Market Value of the Company?

Warren believes that if you can purchase a company with a consumer monopoly working in its favor at the right price, the retained earnings of the business will continuously increase the underlying value of the business and the market will continuously ratchet up the price of a company's stock. A perfect example of this is his own Berkshire Hathaway, which in 1983 had a shareholders' equity of $975 a share and was trading at around $1,000 a share. Seventeen years later, in 2000, it has a shareholders' equity of approximately $38,000 a share and is trading at approximately $50,000. This means that Berkshire's shareholders' equity increased approximately 3,789% and the price of its shares by 4,900% since 1983. Warren grew the company's net worth by using the company's retained earnings to purchase whole or partial interests of businesses that have consumer monopolies. As the net worth of the company grew, so did the market's valuation of the company, thus the rise in the price of the stock.

This is not true with a commodity type business. Such businesses can retain earnings for years and still never show a real increase in the value of the company's stock. In 1983 General Motors had a shareholders' equity of $32.44 a share and was trading at approximately $34. In 2000, General Motors' shareholders' equity stood at approximately $36 a share and the price of its shares at around $70. Seventeen years of business and all General Motors has to show for it is an 11% increase in its shareholders' equity and a 106% increase in the price of its stock.

I'd rather be driving a Berkshire. Wouldn't you?

Though later on in the book we will equip you better to perform this exercise, we want you to now try to list ten companies in which you *believe* the accumulation of retained earnings has caused a corresponding increase in their stock market values. After you have made your list, check out their respective historical market price performance in *Value Line* or on Yahoo! Finance and MSN.com. Were you on the money? Did your picks increase in value as their retained earnings increased?

1. Berkshire Hathaway _____

2. _____

3. _____

4. _____

5. _____

6. _____

7. _____

8. _____

9. _____

10. _____

## Summary

Warren is looking to invest in the business that has excellent economics working in its favor. He discovered that these stellar businesses usually have some kind of consumer monopoly that produces phenomenal profits. Consumer monopolies are usually noted by a brand name product or service that consumers believe offers superior advantages over any of the competition.

Warren wants to own a company with a consumer monopoly that will experience a real increase in its long-term economic value. He invests in that company only if it makes business sense (a topic we address later.) He has found that his best purchases are presented to him when the short-sightedness of the market overreacts to bad news. After he makes his purchase he holds the stock, letting the retained earnings increase the underlying value of the business. The market, seeing the underlying increase in the value of the business, then correspondingly increases the market price of the stock. **This is the method that he has used to create his super wealth. The trick is to find the consumer monopoly and buy it at a cheap price.** In the next chapter we will learn how to go about finding a consumer monopoly to invest in.

# KEY POINTS FROM THIS CHAPTER

- **A consumer monopoly is usually evidenced by a brand name product or key service.**

- **Warren looks for the consumer monopoly to produce earnings that are strong and show an upward trend.**

- **A company that benefits from the high profits that a consumer monopoly produces will usually be conservatively financed. Often it carries no debt at all, which means that it has considerable financial punch to solve problems and to take advantage of new business prospects.**

- **Warren believes that in order for a company to make shareholders rich over the long run it must earn high rates of return on shareholders' equity.**

- **He also believes that the company must be able to retain its earnings and not have to spend it all on maintaining current operations.**

## Study Questions

Why is a high return on shareholders' equity important to Warren?

Why is it important for a company to be able to adjust prices to inflation?

Why is it important that you look for a company that is conservatively financed?

## True or False

1. T or F     Weak and erratic earnings are indicative of the consumer monopoly.

2. T or F     A consumer monopoly is usually conservatively financed.

3.  T or F     A consumer monopoly adds value to the business by retaining earnings.

4.  T or F     A consumer monopoly is free to adjust price to keep pace with inflation.

Answers: 1. False 2. True 3. True 4. True

# 6: WHERE TO LOOK FOR A CONSUMER MONOPOLY

What causes the phenomenon of the consumer monopoly? Why do some businesses earn consistently higher rates of return on invested capital than others? As we discussed earlier, Warren works with a concept that he calls the *toll bridge* effect. If you want to cross a toll bridge, you have to pay the toll. The trick is to find businesses to invest in that have conceptual toll bridges. If you want to use that product or service, you have to pay the toll. Warren has identified four types of toll bridge/consumer monopoly businesses that produce excellent results:

1. Businesses that make products that wear out fast or are used up quickly, that have brand name appeal, and that merchants have to carry or use to stay in business

2. Communications businesses that provide a repetitive service that manufacturers must use to persuade the public to buy their products

3. Businesses that provide repetitive consumer services that people and businesses are consistently in need of

4. Retail stores that have acquired a regional quasi-monopoly position selling such items as jewelry and furniture

Let's examine each of these categories.

## 1. Businesses that make products that wear out fast or are used up quickly, that have brand name appeal, and that merchants have to carry to stay in business

Merchants like the local supermarket, as opposed to manufacturers like the Coca-Cola Company, make their profits by buying low and selling high. The merchant needs to pay as little for a product as possible and sell it for as much as possible. The profit is the difference between what the merchant paid for the product and what he can sell it for. If a product has several manufacturers, a merchant can shift from one to the other, shopping for the lowest price. However, if a product is available from only one manufacturer, then the merchant has to pay the price that manufacturer asks, thus giving the pricing advantage to the manufacturer and not the merchant. This means both higher profit margins and higher profits for the manufacturer.

Note that when a great number of merchants want to sell a particular product supplied exclusively by one manufacturer, the price competition shifts to the merchants. Different merchants cut the price of the product to stimulate sales. *But the manufacturer charges all the merchants the same price.* The price competition *between the merchants* destroys the merchants' profit margins but *not* the manufacturer's.

Companies that manufacture brand name products that are used up quickly, which merchants have to carry to be in business, are, in effect, a kind of toll bridge. The consumer wants a particular brand name product; if the merchant wants to earn a profit, he or she has to supply the consumer with that product. The catch is that there is only one manufacturer (only one bridge) and if you want that brand name product, you have to pay (the toll) *that manufacturer.*

Let's take a trip down to the local Kwik Shop or 7-Eleven. As you stand at the door, can you predict what brand name products you'll find inside? Coca-Cola, Marlboro cigarettes, Skoal chewing tobacco, Hershey's chocolate, Wrigley's chewing gum, and Doritos. Without these products the owner loses sales. The manufacturers of all these products—the Coca-Cola Company, the Philip Morris Company (Marlboro cigarettes), UST (Skoal chewing tobacco), Hershey Foods (Hershey's chocolate), Wm. Wrigley Jr. Company (Wrigley's chewing gum), and the Pepsi-Cola Company (Doritos)—all earn above average rates of return on shareholders' equity.

Think of eight brand name products that every pharmacy has to carry. Here are mine: Crest toothpaste, Advil, Listerine, Coca-Cola, Marlboro cigarettes, Tampax tampons, Bic pens, and Gillette razor blades. Without these products the drugstore merchant is going to lose sales. The manufacturers of all these products earn high returns on shareholders' equity.

When you go out to eat at a restaurant, you don't order your coffee by brand name. Nor do you order your hamburger and fries or BLT or shrimp fried rice or iced tea that way. The company that sells the restaurant hamburger does not earn above average profits on the products it sells, because nobody ever walks into a restaurant and asks for a hamburger from Bob's Meats.

But you order your Coca-Cola by brand name, and if you own a restaurant and you don't carry Coca-Cola, well, you just lost a few customers.

What brand name products must most clothing stores sell? Fruit-of-the-Loom or Hanes underwear, and, of course, the ubiquitous Levi's. Both earn their manufacturers high rates of return on shareholders' equity. How about stores that sell running shoes? Does Nike ring a bell? Nike earns excellent returns on shareholders' equity. How about the corner hardware store? WD-40 and GE lightbulbs. Both of these manufacturers earn—you guessed it—above average returns on shareholders' equity.

Think about the prescription drugs behind the druggist's counter. We live in an age in which an overcrowded planet is connected by thousands of daily international flights. New diseases can jump from one country to another in a matter of hours. Throw in the fact that viruses can mutate into new strains almost overnight and it doesn't take a genius to see that these modern-day potions salesmen, the pharmaceutical companies, are going to have an ever-increasing demand for their lifesaving products. Patented pharmaceuticals that people desperately need are only available to those willing to pay the toll. The gatekeeper, the druggist, has to carry the products or lose business. All of the leading manufacturers of prescription drugs such as Merck & Company, Marion Merrell Dow, Inc., Mylan Labs, and Eli Lilly and Company are very profitable enterprises.

We should take special note of restaurant chains that have created brand name products out of generic food. Restaurant chains, such as McDonald's, have taken the most ubiquitous of food, the hamburger, and turned it into a brand name product. The keys to its success are quality, convenience, consistency, and affordability. Take a bite out of a McDonald's hamburger in Hong Kong and it tastes like the one you bit into the month before in the good old U.S.A. McDonald's consistently earns above average rates of return on shareholders' equity.

Advertising by manufacturers ensures that customers will demand the advertised products and that merchants can't substitute a cheaper product on which they can earn fatter profit margins. The merchant becomes the gatekeeper to the toll bridge, with the manufacturer being guaranteed his profit. Since these products are being consumed either on the spot or within a short period of time thereafter, the gatekeeper and the manufacturer can expect frequent trips across the bridge.

For Warren, the brand name consumer product is the kind of toll bridge business that he is interested in owning.

List ten companies that sell brand name products that wear out or are used up quickly:

1. <u>Sara Lee Corp.</u>

2. _____

3. _____

4. _____

5. _____

6. _____

7. _____

8. _____

9. _____

10. _____

## True or False

1. T or F    Warren is interested in companies that manufacture brand name products that wear out or are used up quickly.

2. T or F    Warren is also interested in companies that have earnings that show a strong upward trend but have suffered a setback in the current year.

3. T or F    Warren is also interested in companies that have erratic earnings.

Answers: 1. True 2. True 3. False

## 2. Communications businesses that provide a repetitive service that manufacturers must use to persuade the public to buy their products

Long ago, the manufacturers of products reached their potential customers by having company salesmen call on customers directly. With the advent of radio, television, newspapers, and a huge number of highly specialized magazines, manufacturers found that they could skip the company salespeople and make their pitch directly to thousands of people with a single well-placed advertisement. Manufacturers found that these new mediums of reaching the customer worked, which meant an increase in sales and profits. Ultimately advertising became the battleground on which manufacturers competed with one another, with huge consumer corporations spending hundreds of millions of dollars a year on getting their "buy-our-product" message to potential customers.

After a while these companies found that there was no turning back. Manufacturers had to advertise or they ran the risk that some competitor would sweep in and take over their coveted niche in the marketplace.

Warren found that advertising created a conceptual bridge between the potential consumer and manufacturer. In order for a manufacturer to create a demand for its product it must advertise. Call it an advertising toll bridge. This advertising toll bridge is owned by the advertising agencies, magazine publishers, newspapers, and telecommunications networks of the world.

When there were only three major TV networks, each one made a great deal of money. Seeing this, Warren invested heavily in ABC and then Capital Cities. Now that there are sixty-seven channels to choose from, the networks don't do as well. They still make a ton of money, just not as much as when there were only three network toll bridges crossing the river.

The same can be said of the newspaper business. A lone newspaper in a good-size town can make excellent returns, but add a competitor and neither will do very well. This is what Warren experienced with the *Buffalo Evening News*. When there was a competitor in town the paper was, at best, an average business. Since the competitor went out of business, the *Buffalo Evening News* has been getting spectacular results. Warren discovered that if there is only one newspaper "toll bridge" in town it can jack its advertising rates to the moon and still not lose customers. Where else are the manufacturers and merchants going to cross the river to reach consumers?

Advertising agencies that function on a worldwide scale also enjoy high returns on shareholders' equity by being in a unique position to profit from the huge multinational companies that want to sell their products all over the world. If one of these multinationals wants to launch an advertising campaign, it has to use an advertising agency like Interpublic, the second-largest in the world. Interpublic becomes the toll bridge to the consumer that the multinational manufacturer must cross. This is the line of reasoning Warren used when he bought 17% of Interpublic.

List ten communications businesses that provide repetitive services that manufacturers must use to persuade the public to buy their products:

1. Gannett Co. _____
2. _____
3. _____
4. _____
5. _____
6. _____
7. _____
8. _____
9. _____
10. _____

## 3. Businesses that provide repetitive consumer services that people and businesses are consistently in need of

These companies provide services, and the services they provide can be performed by nonunion workers, often with limited skills, who are hired on an as-needed basis. This odd segment of the business world includes such companies as Service Master, which provides pest control, professional cleaning, maid service, and lawn care; and Rollins, which runs Orkin, the world's largest pest and termite control service, and also provides security services to homes and businesses. Think about the home security business for a moment. You wire it up and the customer sends you a monthly check, sometimes for the rest of their lives. We all know that at tax time H & R Block is there to save our necks. All of these companies earn high rates of return on shareholders' equity.

This segment of Warren's toll bridge world also includes the credit card companies that he has invested in, such as American Express. This is an interesting kind of business; not only do they charge the merchant a fee every time you use one of these company's cards, they also charge you almost usurious amounts of interest on any unpaid balance you keep with them. Millions of little tolls taxed on each transaction add up. Toss in the interest charges and you will soon see why Warren finds these companies so attractive. These strange credit card toll bridges don't need huge plants or research and development budgets to suck up capital.

The key to these companies is that they provide necessary services but require little in the way of capital expenditures or a highly paid educated workforce. Additionally, there is no such thing as product obsolescence. Once the management and infrastructure are in place, the company can hire and fire employees as the work demand dictates. You hire a person to work as a security guard for $6 an hour, give him a few hours of training, and then rent him out at $25 an hour. When there is no work you don't have to pay him.

Also, no one has to spend money and energy on upgrading or developing new products. The money these companies make goes directly into their pockets and can be spent on expanding operations, paying out dividends, or buying back stock.

List ten businesses that provide repetitive consumer services that people and businesses are consistently in need of:

1. <u>Service Master</u>
2. _____
3. _____
4. _____
5. _____
6. _____
7. _____
8. _____
9. _____
10. _____

## 4. Retail stores that have acquired a regional quasi-monopoly position selling such items as jewelry and furniture

Warren discovered that certain large retailers earn quasi-monopoly profits by selling cheap and moving a lot of inventory. They have branded the store's name to mean quality, good service, and cheap prices and in the process have acquired a great deal of economic goodwill within the community. He found this to be particularly true with large furniture stores that dominate their marketplace, like the Nebraska Furniture Mart owned by Berkshire Hathaway. Their buying power allows them to purchase large quantities of inventory deeply discounted from manufacturers. This in turn allows them to sell cheaper than the competition. This is known as monopoly buying power. The purchaser is so large that it can dictate lower prices for large quantities of goods. The manufacturer makes up for the lower profit margin on each item by selling greater quantities. This is where economics of scale fall into play and into pay, for the manufacturer can earn a bundle on just one huge order. The

Nebraska Furniture Mart can then pass part of the savings on to the customer, thus undercutting the prices of its competitors.

Also these merchants, as a rule, own their stores and the property that they sit on. Thus, the enormous cost of creating a large retail space was paid for years ago—think of it as free rent. Cheaper prices mean happier customers, which means that they keep coming back, which means that the store sells more products and makes more money. This is a classic situation in which low profit margins are okay as long as there is high inventory turnover (you sell a lot of goods.)

These companies create an enormous barrier to entry by being the low-cost operator, carrying large inventories, and selling so cheap. Anyone trying to muscle in on their market would face huge expenses just opening their doors. They would have to finance the acquisition of a large retail space, acquire a huge inventory, and advertise like crazy just to get started. If profit margins were a little higher a competitor might be able to make a beachhead and start to challenge the monopoly positioned retailer, but since profit margins are so very low there is an almost impossible economic barrier to entry.

The same can be said of large jewelry store chains that have an enormous amount of buying power to acquire jewelry at the lowest possible price. They then sell it a price lower than the local mom and pop jewelry store can. They too can create a monopoly type situation that makes it very hard to compete against them. In Warren's home town of Omaha, one store called Borsheim's did manage to compete by doing business out of a cheap downtown location and by selling expensive jewelry cheaper than it could be purchased from, say, Tiffany's in New York City. Local chain stores didn't even try for the top end business, so this one store managed to acquire it all. Word eventually got around that the owner, Ike Friedman, was very honest and would always make you a great deal. Soon people were flying in from out of town just to do business with him. This is an example of a high-end jewelry store working on the theory that you can do great business with lower profit margins and higher volume. Business became so good at Ike's store that Borsheim's became the largest single high-end jewelry store in the world. Warren loved the business so much that he bought the company from Ike in 1986 and has been profiting from the sale of gold, silver, diamonds, and rubies ever since.

As long as the locusts keeping coming, the termites keep eating, the thieves keep thieving, shoppers keep using credit cards, governments keep taxing us, people need beds to sleep in and couches to sit on, and the rich need to rattle their jewels, these companies will make money. Lots of money, for a very, very, very, long time to come.

List five superstores that have acquired monopolylike positions by doing huge volumes of business at discount prices:

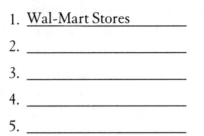

1. Wal-Mart Stores_____

2. _____

3. _____

4. _____

5. _____

## True or False

1. T or F    By selling cheaply and doing large volumes of business it is possible for a retail store to acquire a monopoly-like position.

2. T or F    Monopoly retailers don't usually rely on large volume to make up for poor profit margins.

3. T or F    Monopoly retailers often buy in large quantities to get deep discounts from manufacturers.

4. T or F    Monopoly retailers create a barrier to entry by selling so cheap and keeping their overhead low.

Answers: 1. True 2. False 3. True 4. True

### Summary

The best way to start your search for the excellent business/toll bridge is to stand outside a supermarket or Kwik Shop or 7-Eleven and try to name the brand name products the store must carry to be in business. This mental process is much better than thumbing through endless financial magazines and guides searching for the elusive company of your dreams.

The products that you will come up with will lead you to the companies that are sitting on consumer jackpots of gold, getting high returns on shareholders' equity, and earning superior profits for their owners. So get a pen and paper and start making your list.

Other companies of interest will be those that are uniquely situated to profit from providing advertising services to businesses, like the only newspaper in town.

Of special interest will be those companies that provide repetitive services that require neither products nor skilled labor, like Service Master, Rollins, H & R Block, and American Express.

Not to be missed are those retail stores that have acquired quasi-monopoly positions by way of operating on low margins coupled with high inventory turnover.

Warren found that any one of these types of companies, if purchased at the right price, can lead one to a river of gold.

---

## KEY POINTS
## FROM THIS CHAPTER

- **Warren has discovered that there are basically four types of consumer monopolies:**

  - **Businesses that make products that wear out fast or are used up quickly, that have brand name appeal, and that merchants have to carry or use to stay in business**

  - **Communications businesses that provide a repetitive service that manufacturers must use to persuade the public to buy their products**

  - **Businesses that provide repetitive consumer services that people and business are consistently in need of**

  - **Retail stores that have acquired a quasi-monopoly position selling such items as jewelry and furniture**

---

## Study Questions

Why is it difficult for a merchant to acquire the business characteristics of a consumer monopoly? Why are only a few able to do it?

Why is it important that the brand name products be used up quickly?

Make a list of everyday products that you buy and services that you use and determine whether any of them hold a consumer monopoly position.

## 7: THE BAD NEWS THAT CREATES A BUYING SITUATION

The key to Warren's success is that he invests in consumer monopolies when their stock price has been depressed because of a recent setback in the business—a setback that he is certain the company will recover from. He has identified certain recoverable situations that will cause the stock price of a consumer monopoly to decline. We shall label them *Stock Market Corrections and Panics, Industry Recessions, Individual Calamities,* and *Structural Changes.*

### Stock Market Corrections and Panics

Stock market corrections and panics are easy to spot and usually the safest because they don't tend to change the earnings of the underlying business. That is, unless the company is somehow tied to the investment business, in which case a market downturn tends to reduce general market trading activity, which means brokerage firms and investment banks lose money. Otherwise the underlying economics of most businesses stay the same. *During stock market corrections and panics, stock prices drop for reasons having nothing to do with the underlying economics of their respective companies.*

This is the easiest kind of situation to invest in because there is no real business problem for the company to overcome. If you let the price of the security, as Warren does, determine whether or not the investment gets bought, then this is possibly the safest "buy" situation there is. Warren began buying *The Washington Post* during the stock market crash of '73–'74 and Coca-Cola during the crash of '87. While everyone else was caught in a state of panic, Warren began buying these companies' shares like a man possessed with a deep thirst for value. He eventually acquired 1,727,765 shares of *The Washington Post* and 200,000,000 shares of Coca-Cola.

A market correction or panic will more than likely drive all stock prices down, but it will really hammer those that have recently announced bad news, like a recent decline in earnings. Remember, a market panic accents the effect that bad news has on stock price. **Warren believes that the perfect buying situation can be created when there is a stock market panic coupled with bad news about the company.**

Any company with a strong consumer monopoly will eventually recover after a market correction or panic. **But beware: In a really high market, in which stock prices are trading in excess of forty times earnings, it may take a considerable amount of time for things to recover after a major correction or panic. Companies of the commodity type may never again see their bull market highs, which means investors can suffer a very real and permanent loss of capital.**

After a market correction or panic, stock prices of the consumer monopoly type company will usually rebound within a year or two. This bounce effect will often provide an investor an opportunity to pick up a great price on an exceptional business and see a dramatic profit within a year or two of purchasing the stock. Stock market corrections and panics have made Warren a very happy and a very rich man.

## Industry Recession

The second kind of situation that presents a buying opportunity is an industry-wide recession. In this case an entire industry suffers a financial setback. These situations vary in their intensity and depth. An industry recession can lead to serious losses or it can mean nothing more than mild reduction in per share earnings. Recovery time from this type of situation can be considerable, one to four years, but it does present excellent buying opportunities. In severe examples, a business may even end up in bankruptcy. Don't be fooled by too cheap a selling price. Stay with a well-capitalized leader, one that was very profitable before the recession.

Capital Cities/ABC Inc. fell victim to this weird manic-depressive stock market behavior in 1990. Because of a business recession, advertising revenues started to drop, and Capital Cities reported that its net profit for 1990 would be approximately the same as in 1989. The stock market, used to Capital Cities growing its per share earnings at approximately 27% a year, reacted violently to this news and in the space of six months drove the price of its stock down from $63.30 a share to $38 a share. Thus, Capital Cities lost 40% of its per share price, all because it projected that things were going to be the same as they were last year. (In 1995, Capital Cities and the Walt Disney Company agreed to merge. This caused the market-revalued Capital Cities to upward of $125 a share. If you bought it in 1990 for $38 a share and sold it in 1995 for $125 a share, your pretax annual compounding rate of return would be approximately 26%, with a per share profit of $87.)

Warren used the banking industry recession in 1990 as the impetus for investing in Wells Fargo, an investment that brought him enormous rewards. Remember, in an industry-wide recession, everyone gets hurt. But the strong survive and the weak are removed from the economic landscape. Wells Fargo is one of the most conservative, well run, and financially strong of the key money center banks on the West Coast, and the seventh-largest bank in the nation. (For the sake of clarity in this example we have not adjusted Wells Fargo's historical numbers for splits up to 2000. If you would like to adjust them, divide by six all per share figures.)

Wells Fargo, in 1990 and 1991, responding to a nationwide recession in the real estate market, set aside for potential loan losses a little over $1.3 billion, or approximately $25 a share of its $55 a share in net worth. When a bank sets aside funds for potential losses it is merely designating part of its net worth as a reserve for *potential* future losses. It doesn't mean those losses *have* happened, nor does it mean they *will* happen. What it means is that there is a potential for the losses to occur and that the bank is prepared to meet them.

This means that if Wells Fargo lost every penny it had set aside for potential losses, $25 a share, it would still have $28 a share left in net worth. Losses did eventually occur, but they weren't as bad as Wells Fargo prepared for. In 1991 they wiped out most of Wells Fargo's earnings. But the bank was still very solvent and still reported in 1991 a small net profit of $21 million, or $0.04 a share.

Wall Street reacted as if Wells Fargo was a regional savings and loan on the brink of insolvency, and in the space of four months hammered Wells Fargo's stock price from $86 a share to $41.30 a share. Wells Fargo lost 52% of its per share market price because it essentially was not going to make any money in 1991. Warren responded by buying 10% of the company—or 5 million shares—for an average price of $57.80 a share.

What Warren saw in Wells Fargo was one of the best managed and profitable money-center banks in the country, selling in the stock market for a price that was considerably less than what comparable banks were selling for in the private market. Although all banks compete with each other, as we said, money-center banks like Wells Fargo have a kind of toll bridge monopoly on financial transactions. If you are going to function in society, be it as an individual, a mom and pop business, or a billion-dollar corporation, you need a bank account, a business loan, a car loan, or a mortgage. And with every bank account, business loan, car loan, or mortgage comes the banker charging you fees for the myriad services he provides. California, by the way, has a lot of people, thousands of businesses, and a lot of small and medium size banks, and Wells Fargo is there to serve them all—for a fee.

The loan losses that Wells Fargo anticipated never reached the magnitude expected, and nine years later, in 2000, if you wanted to buy a share of Wells Fargo you would have to have paid approximately $270 a share. Warren ended up with a pretax annual compounding rate of return of approximately 18.6% on his 1991 investment. For Warren there is no business like the banking business.

In the cases of both Capital Cities and Wells Fargo, there was a dramatic drop in their share prices because of an industry-wide recession, which created the opportunity for Warren to make serious investments at bargain prices.

## Individual Calamity

Sometimes brilliant companies do stupid things, and when they do, they lose some very big money. The stock market seeing this, nine out of ten times will slam the stock price. Your job is to figure out whether it is just a passing calamity or something permanent. A company that has the financial power of a consumer monopoly behind it has the strength to survive almost any calamity. Warren first invested in Geico and American Express when they made business blunders that literally cost them their entire net worth.

Occasionally, a company with a great consumer monopoly working in its favor does something that is both stupid and correctable. From 1936 to the mid-1970s Geico made a fortune insuring preferred drivers by operating at low cost and eliminating agents by operating via direct mail. But by the early 1970s, new management had decided that it would try to grow the company further by selling insurance to just about anyone who knocked on its door.

This new philosophy of insuring any and all brought Geico a large number of drivers who were accident prone. More accidents meant that Geico would lose more money, which it did. In 1975 it reported a net loss of $126 million, placing it on the brink of insolvency. In response to this crisis, Geico's board of directors hired Jack Byrne as the new chairman and president. Once on board he approached Warren about investing in the company. Warren had only one concern, and that was whether Geico would drop the unprofitable practice of insuring any and all drivers and return to the time-tested format of just insuring preferred drivers at low cost by direct mail. Byrne said that was the plan and Warren made his investment. Warren initially invested in 1976 and continued to buy shares until 1980. His total investment cost him $45.7 million and in 1996, right before he bought the rest of the company (Berkshire now owns 100% of Geico), his investment had grown to be worth $2.393 billion. This equates to an annual compounding rate of return of approximately 28% for the sixteen-year period.

A different type of event happened to American Express in the mid-1960s. The company, through a warehousing subsidiary, verified the existence of about $60 million worth of tanks filled with salad oil, owned by a commodities dealer, Anthony Deanglis. Deanglis in turn put up the salad oil as collateral for $60 million in loans. When Deanglis failed to pay back the loans, his creditors moved to foreclose on the salad oil. But to the surprise of the creditors, the collateral they had loaned money against didn't exist. Since American Express had inadvertently verified the existence of the nonexistent oil, it was held ultimately responsible to the creditors for their losses. American Express ended up having to pay off the creditors to the tune of approximately $60 million.

This loss essentially sucked out the majority of American Express's shareholders' equity base, and Wall Street responded by slamming its stock into the ground. Warren saw this and reasoned that even if the company lost the majority of its shareholders' equity base, the inherent consumer monopolies of the credit card operations and travelers check business still remained intact. This loss of capital would not cause any *long-term* damage to American Express. Seeing this, Warren invested 40% of Buffett Partnership Ltd.'s investment capital in its stock, thus acquiring for the Buffett partners approximately 5% of American Express's outstanding stock. Two years later the market reappraised the stock upward. Warren sold it and pocketed a cool $20 million profit.

Think of it this way. Say you sued Coca-Cola and in *2001* won a judgment of $3 billion or roughly a little more than what the company is expected to report in net earnings for that year. The stock market, hearing the news of your judgment, would kill Coca-Cola's stock price. In truth, however, this loss would have little or no effect on the amount of money that Coca-Cola would make in *2002*. The intrinsic consumer monopoly Coca-Cola possesses would still be intact. Effectively, your $3 billion judgment would be the same as if Coca-Cola had paid out a dividend of $3 billion in 2001. Instead of paying out the dividends to its shareholders, Coca-Cola would have paid it out to you. In the next year, 2002, Coca-Cola will show a net profit of $3 billion or better. By the time 2005 rolls around, no one will have remembered your 2001 judgment, and the price of Coca-Cola's stock will have risen back to its prejudgment price. How soon they forget!

### Structural Changes

Structural changes in a company often produce special charges against earnings that have negative impact on share prices. Mergers, restructuring, and reorganizing costs can have a very negative impact on net earnings, which translates into lower share prices, which might mean a buying opportunity. Warren's investment in Costco was made after it had suffered negative earnings due to merger and restructuring costs.

There are also situations where structural changes like the conversion from corporate form to partnership form, or the spinning off of a business can have a positive impact on the company's stock price. Warren's investments in Tennaco Offshore and Service Master were based on these companies converting from corporate form to a master partnership. His investment in Sears was based on their decision to spin off of its insurance division Allstate.

### Conclusion

There are four major types of bad news situations that give rise to a prospective investment situation: the stock market correction or panic, the industry recession, the individual calamity, and structural changes. All can have a negative impact on a company's stock price.

---

## KEY POINTS
## FROM THIS CHAPTER

- **Bad news situations come in four basic flavors: Stock market correction or panic, industry recession, individual business calamity, and structural changes.**
- **The perfect buying situation is created when a stock market correction or panic is coupled with an industry recession or individual business calamity.**

---

## Study Questions

Explain why a stock market panic is a safer bet than an individual business calamity.

In an industry recession, why is it important to go with the strongest company in the industry?

## True or False

1. T or F     Stock market panics are the easiest to identify of Warren's four buying situations.

2. T or F     Warren has no interest in companies that are suffering a onetime solvable problem.

3. T or F     In an industry recession buying situation, the strongest companies usually come out way ahead of their weaker brethren after the recession is over.

4. T or F     Stock market panics, when combined with either an industry recession or individual calamity, present poor buying opportunities.

Answers: 1. True 2. False 3. True 4. False

# PART TWO

# Warren Buffett's Intrinsic Value Equations

The intrinsic value equations that you will need in order to evaluate whether an investment has the potential strength to survive and prosper beyond a bad news buying situation, and to determine whether or not an investment makes business sense, are fairly easy to learn.

Before you burst out of the gate and blast away on your calculator, however, you must first establish that the company has some kind of consumer monopoly working in its favor. You must determine whether the company is managed by people who are honest and competent and who function with their shareholders' best interests in mind.

Although Warren believes that it is hard to damage a great consumer monopoly through poor management, poor management can make it difficult for the investor to make a profit. Coca-Cola is a prime example of this phenomenon. Coca-Cola has a fantastic consumer monopoly, but in the '70s it was run by management that seemed uncertain about how to increase the per share value of the business. As a result, the company sat dormant, awaiting more enlightened management. It arrived with the appointment of Roberto Goizueta as Coca-Cola's president in 1980. Goizueta immediately picked up the ball and ran for touchdown after touchdown, which produced an increase in Coca-Cola's per share earnings year after year. That caused the price of the stock to shoot up like a rocket. (Great managers don't live forever, though, and with the passing of Goizueta, Coke's new management dropped the ball, making mistake after mistake, the worst being when the company served up a tainted batch of soda that had to be pulled off the shelves in Belgium and France. This was not good for Coke's European sales and certainly was not good for the price of Coke's shares. But bad news is good news to Warren. So this little downturn in Coke's luck could be viewed, instead, as a possible buying opportunity if the price of the shares goes low enough.)

You, the investor, must figure out whether the company's management has the ability to effectively allocate capital in a profitable fashion. This can be determined with the help of a number of calculations. After the economic nature of the business is determined, you can use several other calculations to determine whether or not its shares are selling at a price that makes business sense.

Fire up your calculator, roll up your sleeves, go get yourself a cup of java, a pencil, and a piece of paper, and let's settle in for some serious number crunching—Warren style!

# 8: FINDING THE COMPANY AND THE NUMBERS

There are a couple of rules and tricks in Warren's game that are very helpful to know. You need to discover, as he has, where to look for a company that has both a consumer monopoly and a stock price that has been beaten down.

At this point you should have an idea of what a consumer monopoly is and how to identify whether a company has one or not. As you will soon see, figuring out what kinds of companies have consumer monopolies is not that difficult. *Finding one that is selling at a discount price is.*

Warren says that you pay a hefty price for a stock market consensus and that the time to invest in a company is when no one else is interested in it. That means that you should never buy into a company on good news. Remember that the stock market buys on good news and sells on bad. If you buy on good news, you are going to pay full price. If you want to buy in at a discount, you have to wait for the negative news.

The first thing you want to avoid is any company that is the popular investment of the day. Warren is interested in unpopular companies, those in which no one else wants to invest.

How important is it to get as low a price as possible? Incredibly important. Many investment analysts and others who write about Buffett's strategies believe that if you are buying an excellent business, one with a consumer monopoly, and you anticipate holding it for a number of years, you needn't be all that concerned about the price you pay. *They're dead wrong.* Consider this. In 1989 Wrigley's traded between $11.80 and $17.90 a share. Ten years later, in 1999, it traded at $100 a share. If you paid $11.80 for a share back in 1989, and sold it for $100 a share in 1999, then your pretax annual compounding rate of return would be approximately **23.8%**. If you paid $17.90 a share in 1989, and sold it for $100 a share in 1999, then your pretax annual compounding rate of return would equate to approximately **18.7%**.

Had you invested **$100,000** in Wrigley back in 1989 when the share price was $17.90, it would have compounded annually at 18.7% and grown to be worth approximately **$555,273.80** by 1999. If you had invested $100,000 in Wrigley at $11.80 a share, back in 1989, it would have compounded annually at 23.8% and grown to be worth approximately **$845,680.75** by 1999. That's a difference of **$290,406.95!** Pay more, earn less. Pay less, earn more.

Remember the Texas Instruments BA-35 Solar financial calculator we told you about in the beginning of the book? Well, this is where you get to use it. The first thing that you do is make sure that the calculator is in its financial mode (hit the Mode key until you'll see a small FIN on the screen). Then punch in Wrigley's 1989 per share market price of $11.80 as the present value (the PV key) and then punch in the number of years, 10 (the N key). Punch in the per share price at which you sold the stock in 1999, $100, as the future value (the FV key). Then hit the calculation key (CPT), and then the interest key (%i). Then the calculator will tell you that your compounding annual rate of return for the ten-year period on your original investment of $11.80 a share is 23.8%.

Warren's rule for price is simple: You want to pay the lowest price possible because ultimately it is going to determine your compounding rate of return and whether or not you are going to get rich.

In order to recognize a low price, you have to keep abreast of what is happening to the company. Warren has an encyclopedic knowledge of more than 1,000 different companies. He can tell you something about each company that trades on the New York Stock Exchange. This doesn't sound all that extraordinary if you consider that as a child one of his favorite pastimes was memorizing the statistics off the back of baseball cards. If you are a mere mortal, the next best thing to having an encyclopedic mind is the Internet.

With the click of a mouse the Internet provides the individual investor with a wealth of information that once took weeks to assemble. The financial Web pages post daily reports on what companies are having problems and what stocks are suffering from a sell-off. For example, MSN.com's financial page keeps track of what's hot and is not by industry and by individual company. Yahoo! does the same thing. Detecting which companies have fallen from grace is not as difficult as it used to be. Simply check out a financial Web page every day and see what is going on. They usually list ten stocks that have fallen out. Check out each and every company. Most of these Web sites will also provide you with the financials and a host of other ratios and numbers on these businesses. Additionally, they will link you up with the corresponding SEC documentation as well as a link to the company's Web site. Plus, they will give you access to all recent news stories about the company. You should know that through the EDGAR reporting system, the SEC maintains financial records on every company publicly traded in the United States. This is an excellent source of information, as we said, that is just a few clicks of a mouse away.

If the company you are interested in has a Web site, make certain to visit it. There you will usually find a copy of the company's annual report and other pertinent financial information. You should also find a detailed description of what the company does. Read it. You'll see whether it's a commodity or consumer monopoly type business.

Warren has subscribed to the *Value Line Investment Survey* for years. It provides you with about fifteen years' worth of past financial numbers for about 1,600 different companies. You should give this a periodic thumbing through. If you can't afford the subscription price, your local library should have a copy you can consult for free. If you don't own a computer, the local library should be able to provide you with free access to the Internet as well. You can also phone the head office of the company you are interested in to get a free copy of its annual report.

Once you have focused on a company that looks interesting, and have assembled the appropriate information (current balance sheet, income statement, and the per share earnings and return on shareholders' equity figures for a ten-year period), you can start running the intrinsic value equations that Warren uses to determine the earning power of a company. You do this to determine two things: the first is whether the company in question has a consumer monopoly, and if it does, just how powerful it is. The second is whether the company in question is selling at a price that makes business sense, which usually happens when either the stock market or the company is experiencing some kind of calamity.

---

### KEY POINTS
### FROM THIS CHAPTER

- You can get all the information you need for analysis purposes off the Internet free!

- A "What's Hot and What's Not" list on the Internet is a good place to start hunting for a buying situation.

- The SEC through its EDGAR system maintains financial records on every company that is publicly traded on the Internet. You can access their records on-line at www.freeedgar.com.

- The price you pay ultimately determines your annual compounding rate of return.

---

## Study Questions

Name four Internet sites that you can use to obtain information about a company.

1.    Yahoo! Financial

2.    _____

3.    _____

4.    _____

What financial records do you need to assemble before you can begin your process of analysis?

1.    _____

2.    _____

3.    _____

4.    _____

Answers: 1. current balance sheet 2. income statement
3. the per share earnings for a ten-year period
4. return on shareholders' equity figures for a ten-year period

# 9: FINANCIAL CALCULATION #1: PREDICTABILITY OF EARNINGS AT A GLANCE

Warren has found that without some predictability about a company's future earnings, it is impossible to tell whether the company will have the strength to survive the bad news that gave rise to the buying situation in the first place. The following test is the simplest test you can perform and it is probably the most basic. It gives you an instant perspective on whether or not the company has predictable earnings. Although every security analyst performs this calculation, the first time his or her eyes scan an investment survey like *Moody's* or *Value Line,* few will acknowledge that it is an actual calculation. But it is, because it is where you must start the process of statistical analysis. Simply put, it means comparing the reported per share earnings for a number of years against one another. Are they consistent or inconsistent? Do earnings trend upward or do they climb and then plunge down like a roller coaster? Are they strong? Do they indicate a loss or earnings weakness in the current year?

Investment survey services, such as *Moody's* and *Value Line,* make this comparison of yearly figures very easy by providing you with a list of earnings dating back several years. So does the MSN.com Web site, the Yahoo! Financial Web site, and about a dozen others. We are an investing nation awash in financial figures.

## THE FOUR TYPES OF EARNINGS SITUATIONS THAT YOU WILL CONFRONT

As you peruse various companies' earnings, you will confront four different types of earnings situations—three that interest us and one that does not. Ideally, the company's per share earnings are consistently strong and show an upward trend as shown in Exhibit A for Company I. The company that we are definitely not interested in is one in which earnings are wildly erratic, as is shown in Exhibit A as Company II.

### EXHIBIT A

### COMPANY I
### Consumer Monopoly Type Business

| Year | Per Share Earnings |
|------|--------------------|
| 1990 | $1.07 |
| 1991 | $1.16 |
| 1992 | $1.28 |
| 1993 | $1.42 |
| 1994 | $1.64 |
| 1995 | $1.60 |
| 1996 | $1.90 |
| 1997 | $2.39 |
| 1998 | $2.43 |
| 1999 | $2.69 |

### COMPANY II
### Commodity Type Business

| Year | Per Share Earnings |
|------|--------------------|
| 1990 | $1.57 |
| 1991 | $0.16 |
| 1992 | $(1.28) loss |
| 1993 | $0.42 |
| 1994 | $(0.23) loss |
| 1995 | $0.60 |
| 1996 | $1.90 |
| 1997 | $2.39 |
| 1998 | $(0.43) loss |
| 1999 | $0.69 |

Company I has more predictable earnings than Company II. You don't need to be a genius to see that. You can see that per share earnings at Company I have increased every year but 1995, in which there was a drop from $1.64 to $1.60 a share. Company II's earnings, on the other hand, are all over the place, with no apparent trend.

Fast question. Could you predict future earnings for either? Well, you would certainly feel more confident about Company I. Even though all you know about the company is its past ten years of earnings, you know that they are 1) strong and 2) have an upward trend. Your next question should be, "What were the economic dynamics that created this situation?"

Company II might have some investment merit, but from Buffett's point of view, the lack of strong earnings indicates that Company II's future earnings would be impossible to predict with any degree of comfort. At first glance Warren would only have considered Company I.

Warren's mentor, Benjamin Graham, was fond of saying that you don't need to know someone's weight to know that he is fat. The same holds true in reviewing the earnings history of a company. The first thing you should do when investigating the earnings history of a company is gather the per share earnings figures for the last seven to ten years to determine whether they present a stable or unstable picture. There will be a lot of black-and-white examples, but also quite a few that fall into a gray area. If something seems fishy, don't be afraid to move on. If something smells interesting, don't be afraid to dig a little deeper.

## APPLICATION OF EARNINGS PREDICTABILITY TO A NEGATIVE EARNINGS SITUATION AT A GLANCE

In some bad news situations, the per share earnings will have suffered a setback in the current year. That setback may be no more than a weak performance compared to the year before or it may be serious enough to produce an actual loss.

Company III is a perfect example of the type of situation in which the company in question has produced a substantially weaker performance in 1999 than in 1998. Company IV shows a setback that produced a negative result.

## COMPANY III
## Possible Consumer Monopoly in Trouble

| Year | Per Share Earnings |
|------|--------------------|
| 1990 | $1.07 |
| 1991 | $1.16 |
| 1992 | $1.28 |
| 1993 | $1.42 |
| 1994 | $1.64 |
| 1995 | $1.60 |
| 1996 | $1.90 |
| 1997 | $2.39 |
| 1998 | $2.43 |
| 1999 | $.48 → Sharp decline |

## COMPANY IV
## Possible Consumer Monopoly in Trouble

| Year | Per Share Earnings |
|------|--------------------|
| 1990 | $(1.07) |
| 1991 | $1.16 |
| 1992 | $1.28 |
| 1993 | $1.42 |
| 1994 | $1.64 |
| 1995 | $1.60 |
| 1996 | $1.90 |
| 1997 | $2.39 |
| 1998 | $2.43 |
| 1999 | $(1.69) → Actual loss |

Both Company III and Company IV have earnings that are strong, consistent, and growing until 1999. The question is whether or not this an aberration or the way of things to come. The only way to find out is by putting on your analyst's hat and delving into the recent history of the company. If the companies have consumer monopolies working in their favor, you have to figure out whether they are strong enough to overcome the business hurdles that have hurt these companies' earnings. Warren believes that in situations like these, where the potential exists for making huge sums of money, your job is to figure out whether the current situation is permanent or is something that management or the economic environment can correct over time.

# KEY POINTS
# FROM THIS CHAPTER

- **Merely looking at a ten-year summary of a company's per share earnings will tell you a great deal about a company.**

- **Warren is looking for a company that has shown a strong upward trend in per share earnings over the last ten years.**

- **He is not interested in companies that have wildly fluctuating earnings.**

- **He is interested in companies with histories of strong per share earnings that have suffered temporary setbacks in the most recent year.**

## Study Questions

Why might Warren be interested in a company even though it has lost money in the current year?

Why is it important to see a strong upward trend in earnings?

Find and list five companies that show a strong upward trend in earnings.

1.   <u>Abbott Labs</u>

2.   _____

3.   _____

4.   _____

5.   _____

## True or False

1.   T or F     Warren is interested in companies that have earnings that show a strong upward trend.

2.   T or F     Warren is also interested in companies

that have earnings that show a strong
upward trend but have suffered a setback
in the current year.

3.  T or F      Warren is also interested in companies
that have erratic earnings.

# 10: FINANCIAL CALCULATION #2: A TEST TO DETERMINE YOUR INITIAL RATE OF RETURN

**B**efore we go any further, understand that Warren invests from what he calls a "business perspective." This means that he views the earnings of a company in which he has invested as his own in proportion to his ownership in the company. So if a company earns $5 a share and Warren owns 100 shares of the company, he figures that he has just earned $500 ($5 × 100 = $500).

Warren also believes that this company has the choice of either paying that $500 out to him via a dividend or can retain those earnings and reinvest them for him, thus increasing the underlying value of the company. Warren believes that the stock market will, over a period of time, acknowledge this increase in the company's underlying value and cause the stock's price to increase.

This differs from the view that most Wall Street professionals hold. They don't consider the company's earnings their own until they are paid out as dividends. In the early '80s the stock of Warren's holding company, Berkshire Hathaway, traded at $450 a share. Today it trades at around $54,000 a share and has never paid a dividend. The increase in the market price of the stock came from an increase in the underlying value of the company brought about by Warren's profitable reinvestment of Berkshire's retained earnings.

Since Warren considers the earnings to be his, in proportion to the number of shares that he owns, it is possible to determine the *initial* rate of return he can expect to get at a particular trading price.

In 1979 Capital Cities was trading at $3.80 a share against estimated earnings for the year of $0.46 a share. If you paid $3.80 for a share of Capital

Cities stock in '79, your initial rate of return would be 12.1% ($0.46 ÷ $3.80 = 12.1%).

With Warren's 1988 purchase of Coca-Cola stock at $5.22 a share, against 1988 earnings of $0.36 a share, he calculated his initial rate of return to be 6.89% ($0.36 ÷ $5.22 = 6.89%).

This is where Warren and Graham initially derive the theory that the price you pay will determine your rate of return. If Warren had paid $10 a share for his Coca-Cola stock in 1988, instead of $5.22, he would have seen his initial rate of return drop to 3.6%. The higher the price, the lower the rate of return. The lower the price, the higher the rate of return. You want the highest possible rate of return, which is obtained by paying the lowest possible price.

## KEY POINTS FROM THIS CHAPTER

- **Warren has an unorthodox view of a company's earnings. He considers them his in direct proportion to his ownership interest in the company. If the company earns $5 a share and he owns 100 shares, then, as he sees it, he has earned $500.**

- **Warren believes that if you paid $25 a share for a stock that was earning $5 a share, you would be getting an initial rate of return of 20% ($5 ÷ $25 = 20%).**

- **The price you pay determines your rate of return.**

## Study Questions

1. If the company in which you are investing has earnings of $10 a share and you pay $100 a share for it, how would Warren calculate your initial rate of return? _____

2. T or F  If a company's earnings are growing at 15% a year and your initial rate of return is 10%, Warren consider this an equity/bond with an initial rate of return of 10% that will increase by 15% a year.

Answers: 1. 10% 2. True.

# 11: FINANCIAL CALCULATION #3: TEST FOR DETERMINING THE PER SHARE GROWTH RATE

Management's ability to grow the per share earnings of a company is key to growth of the shareholders' value in the company. In order to get per share earnings to grow, the company must employ its retained earnings in a manner that will generate more earnings per share. The increase in per share earnings will, over a period of time, increase the market valuation for the company's stock.

A really fast and easy mathematical method of checking the company's ability to increase per share earnings is to figure the annual compounded rate of growth of the company's per share earnings for the last ten years and the last five years. This will show you the annual compounding rate of earnings growth over the long and short run. We use the two numbers to allow us to see the true long-term nature of the company and to determine whether management's near-term performance has been in line with the long-term.

We'll start with some examples and then do the in-depth analysis. Here are the yearly per share earnings of the newspaper giant Gannett Co., Inc:

## EARNINGS FOR GANNETT CO. FROM 1990 TO 2000

| Year | Per Share Earnings |
|------|--------------------|
| 1990 | $1.18 → Present Value |
| 1991 | $1.00 |
| 1992 | $1.20 |
| 1993 | $1.36 |
| 1994 | $1.62 |
| 1995 | $1.71 |
| 1996 | $1.89 |
| 1997 | $2.50 |
| 1998 | $2.86 |
| 1999 | $3.30 |
| 2000 | $3.70 → Future Value |

Get out your TI BA-35 Solar financial calculator. To calculate the company's per share earnings annual compounding growth rate, treat the first year as your present value, in this case 1990's earnings of $1.18. Then use 2000's earnings of $3.70 as the future value. The number of years is ten. While your TI calculator is in financial mode, punch in $1.18 and press the present value key (PV), punch in $3.70 as the future value and press the future value key (FV), now punch 10 as the number of years, press the number of years key (N) and hit the CPT key followed by the %i key. You will get the annual compounding rate of growth for the ten years, which is 12.1%.

Do the same for the five-year period from 1995 to 2000, using as the present value 1995's earnings of $1.71. The future value will be the earnings for 2000, $3.70. Five is the number of years. Punch the CPT key followed by the %i key and the calculator will tell you that your annual compounding rate of growth was 16.6% for the five-year period between 1995 and 2000.

These two numbers tell you several different things. The first is that the company has had a higher rate of earnings growth in the last five years than it did in the ten-year period from 1990 to 2000. The question you need to ask is: What were the business economics that caused this change? Was Gannett buying up its own stock, or was it investing in profitable new business ventures? Or was it simply seeing an increase in advertising revenue with a corresponding increase in profits?

## Adapting the Per Share Growth Rate to a Negative Earnings Situation

You are going to confront situations in which the company in question shows every indication of having very strong earnings growth for a number of years, but whose per share earnings in the most recent years either show a sharp decline or are otherwise negative as shown in the following example.

### COMPANY I
### Possible Consumer Monopoly in Trouble

| Year | Per Share Earnings |
|------|--------------------|
| 1989 | $0.95 → Present Value |
| 1990 | $1.07 |
| 1991 | $1.16 |
| 1992 | $1.28 |
| 1993 | $1.42 |
| 1994 | $1.64 |
| 1995 | $1.60 |
| 1996 | $1.90 |
| 1997 | $2.39 |
| 1998 | $2.43 |
| 1999 | $2.70 → Future value |
| 2000 | $0.48 → Exclude this year |

### COMPANY II
### Possible Consumer Monopoly in Trouble

| Year | Per Share Earnings |
|------|--------------------|
| 1989 | $0.95 → Present Value |
| 1990 | $1.07 |
| 1991 | $1.16 |
| 1992 | $1.28 |
| 1993 | $1.42 |
| 1994 | $1.64 |
| 1995 | $1.60 |
| 1996 | $1.90 |
| 1997 | $2.39 |
| 1998 | $2.43 |
| 1999 | $2.70 → Future value |
| 2000 | $1.43 (loss) → Exclude this year |

How do you determine the per share growth rate in these situations? It all depends on your analysis of the situation. If you find that the business condition that precipitated the earnings drop will most certainly pass, then one can safely rule out the setback year in the equation. Simply move your present value starting point back one year. Thus, with companies I and II we would use 1989's earnings of $0.95 per share and 1999's earnings of $2.70 as the future value. The span of time that you are examining is still ten years. The annual compounding growth rate is approximately 11%. You should only cancel out the most recent year if you're sure that the situation that has created the problem is solvable and not life threatening to the business. (Note: You could use eight or nine years as the number of years. But you should never use fewer than seven.)

# Study Question

Using the exercise below, pick five companies and determine the consistency and growth for per share earnings for the last ten years. This information can be retrieved from *Value Line*, MSN.com, or Yahoo! Finance.

### Exercise to Determine Per Share Earnings Consistency and Growth Rate

Pick five companies that you believe have consumer monopolies working in their favor and calculate their per share earnings growth rate using the following exercise from *Value Line* or your favorite financial Web site.

| Year | | | Per Share Earnings |
|------|------|------|--------------------|
| 1. <u>1990</u> | | \_\_\_\_ | → **Present value (base year)** |
| 2. <u>1991</u> | one | \_\_\_\_ | Financial Calculation for use with TI BA-35 Solar |
| 3. <u>1992</u> | two | \_\_\_\_ | Calculator: **Earnings per share growth rate.** |
| 4. <u>1993</u> | three | \_\_\_\_ | Use 1990 per share earnings as your present |
| 5. <u>1994</u> | four | \_\_\_\_ | value (PV); 2000 as your future value (FV); |
| 6. <u>1995</u> | five | \_\_\_\_ | and 10 (N) as the number of years. Hit the compute |
| 7. <u>1996</u> | six | \_\_\_\_ | key (CPT) and then the interest key (%i) and your |
| 8. <u>1997</u> | seven | \_\_\_\_ | annual compounding growth rate for per share will |
| 9. <u>1998</u> | eight | \_\_\_\_ | be calculated. |
| 10. <u>1999</u> | nine | \_\_\_\_ | |
| 11. <u>2000</u> | ten | \_\_\_\_ | → **Future value** |

↑

**Number of Years Out from Base Year**

If you want to calculate the earnings growth rate for the last five years, just use 1995 as the base year, 2000 as the future value, and 5 as the number of years (N).

| <u>**Name of Company**</u> | | <u>**Per Share Growth Rate**</u> |
| --- | --- | --- |
| 1. | Abbott Labs | 13.5% for the last ten years |
| 2. | | |
| 3. | | |
| 4. | | |
| 5. | | |

---

# KEY POINTS
# FROM THIS CHAPTER

- **Management's ability to grow per share earnings is the key to growth in share price.**

- **In order to grow per share earnings, the company must employ its retained earnings in a manner that will generate more earnings per share.**

- **The increase in per share earnings will, over a period of time, increase the market valuation for the company's stock.**

## 12: FINANCIAL CALCULATION #4: RELATIVE VALUE TO TREASURY BONDS

**W**arren believes that all investments compete with one another and that rate of return on treasury bonds is the benchmark that all investments must ultimately compete with. A way of establishing the value of the company relative to treasury bonds is to divide the current per share earnings by the current rate of return for treasury bonds. This allows you to compare the rate of return that the company is earning compared to the rate of return on treasury bonds.

In the case of Warren's investment in Capital Cities in 1979, the per share earnings were $0.47 a share. Divide $0.47 a share by the rate of return on treasury bonds, which was approximately 10% in 1979, and you get a relative value of $4.70 a share ($0.47 ÷ .10 = $4.70). This means that if you paid $4.70 for a share of Capital Cities, you would be getting a return equal to that of the treasury bonds—10%. This means that Capital Cities has a value relative to treasury bonds of $4.70 a share.

In 1979 you could have bought Capital Cities stock for less than $4.70 a share. (In fact, the stock traded in a price range of between $3.60 and $4.70 a share. This means that you could have bought the stock at a price that was below its relative value to the return being paid a treasury bonds in 1979. Your rate of return would have been greater than 10%.) Now from 1970 to 1979, the annual per share earnings growth rate for Capital Cities was 20%.

Thus, you can ask yourself this question: What would I rather own— $4.70 worth of a treasury bond with a static rate of return of 10%, or a Capital Cities equity/bond with a return of 10% or better, whose per share earnings are growing at an annual rate of 20%? In fact you may not want to own either, but given a choice between the two, the Capital Cities equity/bond has more enticing qualities.

Many analysts believe that if you divide the per share earnings by the current rate of return on treasury bonds you end up with the intrinsic value of the company. But really all you end up with is the value of the company relative to the return on treasury bonds.

The same thing applies to the theory that the intrinsic value of a business is its future earnings discounted to present value. If you use the rate of return on treasury bonds to determine the discount rate (as most analysts do), all you end up with is a discounted present value relative to the rate of return on treasury bonds.

Remember that the return on treasury bonds is a pre–income tax return and the net earnings figure of a corporation is an after–corporate tax return. So comparing the two without taking this into account is folly. Still, comparing these figures has a place in our box of financial calculations.

## KEY POINTS FROM THIS CHAPTER

- **All investments compete with one another for the investor's capital.**
- **Ultimately the safest investment is a United States Treasury Bond.**
- **The yield on a treasury bond competes with the return paid on other investments.**
- **One can obtain a business perspective by comparing the relative value of one investment to the return paid on a treasury bond.**

## Study Questions

Why would Warren be interested in comparing the returns on different investments?

Why would he want to compare them to the return being paid on treasury bonds?

Pick five companies and determine their relative value to the rate of return being paid on treasury bonds and then compare it their current market price. Use *Value Line,* MSN.com, or Yahoo! Finance to get your initial numbers.

| | Name of Company | Per Share Earnings | | Return on Treasury Bonds | | Relative Value | Current Market Price |
|---|---|---|---|---|---|---|---|
| 1. | Hershey Foods | $2.35 | ÷ | 7% | = | $33.57 | $43 |
| 2. | _____ | _____ | ÷ | _____ | = | _____ | _____ |
| 3. | _____ | _____ | ÷ | _____ | = | _____ | _____ |
| 4. | _____ | _____ | ÷ | _____ | = | _____ | _____ |
| 5. | _____ | _____ | ÷ | _____ | = | _____ | _____ |

# 13: FINANCIAL CALCULATION #5: UNDERSTANDING WARREN'S PREFERENCE FOR COMPANIES THAT EARN HIGH RATES OF RETURN ON SHAREHOLDERS' EQUITY

To understand Warren's preference for businesses that have high returns on shareholders' equity, you must understand that he is of the opinion that consumer monopolies have such consistent earnings that their stocks become a sort of bond. He calls the stock an equity/bond and it pays an interest rate equal to the yearly return on equity that the business is earning. The earnings per share figure is the equity/bond's yield. If the company has a shareholders' equity value of $10 a share and net earnings of $2.50 a share, Warren would say that the company is getting a return on its equity/bond of 25% ($2.50 ÷ $10 = 25%).

But, since a business's earnings are given to fluctuation, the return on the equity/bond is not a fixed figure as it is with other bonds. Warren believes that with an equity/bond, one is buying a variable rate of return, a positive for the investor if earnings increase, and a negative if earnings decrease. The return on the equity/bond will fluctuate as the relationship of shareholders' equity to net earnings changes.

To fully understand why Warren is so interested in high returns on shareholders' equity, let us work deeper into a hypothetical situation we presented earlier in the book.

Remember that shareholders' equity is defined as a company's total assets *less the company's total liabilities*. This is comparable to the equity you hold in your house. Let's say that you bought a house as a rental property and you paid $200,000. To close the deal you invested $50,000 of your own money and borrowed $150,000 from a bank. The $50,000 you invested in the house is your equity in the property.

When you rent out your house, the amount of money you earn, after paying your expenses and mortgage, would be your return on equity. If you rented your house for $15,000 a year and had $10,000 in expenses, mortgage payments, and taxes, then your net earnings would be $5,000 a year. Then the return on your $50,000 in equity would be the $5,000 you earned. This amounts to an annual 10% return on equity ($5,000 ÷ $50,000 = 10%).

Likewise, if you owned a business—we will call it Company A—with $10 million in assets and $4 million liabilities, the business would have shareholders' equity of $6 million. If the company earned, after taxes, $1,980,000, we could calculate the business's return on shareholders' equity as 33% ($1,980,000 ÷ $6,000,000 = 33%). So the $6 million of shareholders' equity is earning a 33% rate of return. (Warren's Company A's equity/bond would also be earning a 33% return on equity.)

Imagine that you owned another business. Call it Company B. Imagine that it too has $10 million in assets and $4 million in liabilities, which, like Company A, gives it $6 million in shareholders' equity. But imagine that instead of making $1,980,000 on an equity base of $6 million, it only makes $480,000. This means that Company B would be producing a return on equity of 8% ($480,000 ÷ $6,000,000 = 8%).

| | Company A | Company B |
|---|---|---|
| Assets | $10 million | $10 million |
| Liabilities | $4 million | $4 million |
| Shareholders' Equity | $6 million | $6 million |
| After Tax Earnings | $1,980,000 | $480,000 |
| Return on Shareholders' Equity | 33% | 8% |

Both companies have exactly the same capital structure, yet Company A is four times as profitable as Company B. Based on this quick assessment, the better company is Company A.

Let's say that the management teams at both Company A and Company B are really good at what they do. Company A's management is really good at getting a 33% return on equity and Company B's is really good at getting an 8% return on equity.

Which company would you rather invest your money in—Company A, whose management will earn you a 33% return on your newly invested money, or Company B, whose management will only earn you an 8% return? You, of course, would choose to invest in Company A, whose management is going to earn you a 33% return.

As the owner of Company A, you have the choice of either getting a $1,980,000 dividend from Company A at the end of the year, or you can let Company A retain your earnings and let its management earn you a 33% return. What do you do? Do you take the dividend or do you let Company A's management continue earning you a 33% return? Is earning a 33% rate of return sufficient? Of course it is. Company A is making you very rich. So you let it keep the money.

As the owner of Company B, you also have the choice of getting either a $480,000 dividend at the end of the year or you can let Company B retain your earnings and let the management earn you an 8% return. Do you take the 8% return? Is an 8% rate of return sufficient enough for you? The decision isn't as easy as it was with Company A. Let me ask you this: If I told you that you could take Company B's dividend and reinvest it in Company A, will that help you make up your mind? Of course it would. You would take your money out of Company B, where it was only earning an 8% rate of return, and reinvest it in Company A, where it would earn a rate of return of 33%.

By now you can start to see why companies that earn high returns on shareholders' equity are big on Warren's list. But there are a few more twists to the wealth-creating power that high returns on equity will produce. Let's look deeper.

Pretend that you don't own either Company A or Company B. Easy enough. Instead you are looking for a business to buy. So you approach the owners of Company A and Company B and ask them if they are interested in selling.

Warren believes that all rates of return ultimately compete with the rate of return paid on treasury bonds. He believes that the government's power to tax ensures the bonds' safety and that investors are very aware of that. This competition of rates, according to Warren, is one of the main reasons that the stock market goes down when interest rates go up and why the stock market goes up when interest rates go down. A stock investment that offers a 10% rate of return is far more enticing than a government bond offering a 5% rate of return. But jack up interest rates to the point that the government bond is offering you a 12% rate of return and the stock's rate of return of 10% suddenly loses its appeal.

With this in mind, the owners of Companies A and B compare what they could earn by selling their businesses and putting their capital into treasury bonds. They could forget about the hassles of owning a business and still earn the same amount of money by investing the proceeds from the sale in bonds. Let's say that at the time you made your offer, government bonds were earning an 8% rate of return.

In the case of Company A, which is earning $1.98 million a year, it would take $24.75 million worth of government bonds to generate $1.98 million in interest. So the owner of Company A tells you that he will sell you the company for $24.75 million. If you pay $24.75 million for Company A you would be paying roughly four times shareholders' equity of $6 million, or 12.5 times its current earnings of $1.98 million.

In the case of Company B, which is earning $480,000 a year, it would take $6 million worth of government bonds to generate $480,000 in interest. So the owner of Company B says that he will sell you his company for $6 million. This means that if you pay $6 million for Company B, you will be paying one time shareholders' equity of $6 million, or 12.5 times Company B's current earnings of $480,000.

Two companies, A and B, both with the same capital structure, but A is worth, relative to the return on government bonds, $24.75 million, and B is worth $6 million. If you paid $24.75 million for Company A, you could expect a return of 8% in your first year of ownership ($1,980,000 divided by $24,750,000 = 0.08). If you paid $6 million for Company B, you could also expect an 8% return in your first year of ownership ($480,000 ÷ $6,000,000 = 0.08).

One of the keys to understanding Warren is realizing that he is not very interested in what a company will be earning next year. What he is interested in is **what the company will be earning in ten years.** While Wall Street is focused on the current situation, Warren realizes that to let the power of the consumer monopoly and compounding work their wonders, he has to focus on the long term. This is why companies that have consumer monopolies and earn high rates of return on shareholder equity are so very important to him.

Look at how Warren might view this situation:

Warren would find Company A far more enticing than Company B. The economics of Company A are such that it can earn a 33% return on shareholders' equity. If management can keep this up, the retained earnings will earn 33% as well. Every year the shareholders' equity pot is going to grow. **It is the growing equity pot and the earnings that go with it that interest Warren.** Let us show you.

| Year | Equity Base* | R.O.E.** | Earnings *** |
|------|-------------|----------|--------------|
| 1 | $  6,000,000 | 33% | $ 1,980,000 |
| 2 | 7,980,000 | 33% | 2,633,400 |
| 3 | 10,613,400 | 33% | 3,502,422 |
| 4 | 14,115,822 | 33% | 4,658,221 |
| 5 | 18,774,043 | 33% | 6,195,434 |
| 6 | 24,960,478 | 33% | 8,239,927 |

| 7 | 33,209,405 | 33% | 10,959,104 |
| 8 | 44,168,509 | 33% | 14,575,608 |
| 9 | 58,744,117 | 33% | 19,385,559 |
| 10 | 78,129,675 | 33% | 25,782,793 |
| 11 | 103,912,470 | 33% | 34,291,115 |

\* Beginning year equity base

\*\* Return on equity

\*\*\* Added to next year's equity base

What you are seeing is the shareholders' equity base compounding at a 33% rate of return. (Remember that Warren is after the highest compounding rate of return possible.)

By the beginning of Year 11, Company A will have a shareholders' equity base of $103,912,470 and expected Year 11 earnings of $34,291,115. If treasury bonds are still at 8% it would take $428 million in government bonds to produce $34,291,115.

If you paid $24.75 million for Company A at the beginning of Year 1 and sold at the beginning of the eleventh year, effectively holding the investment for a full ten years, for $428 million, the amount of treasury bonds that it would take to earn the $34,291,115 that Company A is projected to earn in Year 11, your annual compounding rate of return on your investment would be 33%—a very much nicer number to put in the bank.

The economics of Company B are such that it can only earn an 8% return on shareholders' equity. This means that if management keeps this up the retained earnings will only earn 8% as well. Which means that every year the shareholders' equity pot is going to grow by 8%.

| Year | Equity Base* | R.O.E.** | Earnings *** |
|------|-------------|----------|--------------|
| 1 | $ 6,000,000 | 8% | $ 480,000 |
| 2 | 6,480,000 | 8% | 520,000 |
| 3 | 7,000,000 | 8% | 560,000 |
| 4 | 7,560,000 | 8% | 600,000 |
| 5 | 8,160,000 | 8% | 650,000 |
| 6 | 8,820,000 | 8% | 710,000 |
| 7 | 9,520,000 | 8% | 760,000 |
| 8 | 10,280,000 | 8% | 820,000 |
| 9 | 11,110,000 | 8% | 890,000 |
| 10 | 11,990,000 | 8% | 960,000 |
| 11 | 12,950,000 | 8% | 1,036,000 |

\* Beginning year equity base

\*\* Return on equity

\*\*\* Added to next year's equity base

By the beginning of Year 11, Company B will have a shareholders' equity base of $12,950,000 and expected Year 11 earnings of $1,036,000. If government bonds were still paying 8%, it would take $12.95 million in government bonds to produce $1,036,000.

If you paid $6 million for Company B at the beginning of Year 1 and sold at the beginning of the eleventh year, effectively holding the investment for a full ten years, for $12.95 million, the amount of treasury bonds that it would take to earn the $1,036,000 that Company B is projected to earn in Year 11, your annual compounding rate of return on your investment would be 8%—not such a great number.

Suppose you only have $6,187,500, and you think to yourself, wouldn't it be better to spend it buying all of Company B instead of spending it to buy 25% of Company A? Warren has figured out that even 25% of Company A is a better investment than owning 100% of Company B. If you paid $6,187,500 to buy 25% of Company A and you sold it in the beginning of the 11th year for 25% of A's equivalent treasury bond value—$107 million—your annual compounding rate of return would remain 33%.

You may have realized by now that paying $24.75 million, or 12.5 times earnings, for Company A is a fantastic deal if you expected to be earning a 33% annual compounding rate of return for ten years. In fact, Company A may be worth a lot more. The question that Warren must address is how much more? Let's figure it out.

Say that instead of paying $24.7 million, or 12.5 times earnings, for Company A, you paid $59.4 million, or thirty times Company A's Year 1 earnings of $1.98 million. And let's say you sold it at the beginning of Year 11, which means that you effectively held the investment for ten years, for 12.5 times Year 11's projected earnings of $34,291,115, which equates to ($34,291,115 × 12.5 = $428,638,937). If you paid $59.4 million, or thirty times earnings, for Company A in Year 1, and sold it ten years later for $428,638,937, then your annual compounding rate of return would be 21.8%.

If you paid forty times Company A's Year 1 earnings—$79.2 million—and then sold Company A in ten years for $428,638,937, your annual compounding rate of return would be 18.3%. That's an annual compounding rate of return for ten years that most investment managers can only dream about.

**Very Important Point:** Warren knows a secret: Excellent businesses that benefit from a consumer monopoly, and can consistently earn high rates of return on retained earnings (shareholders' equity), are often bargain buys at what seem to be very high price-to-earnings ratios.

We know that some of you are thinking this is just a hypothetical and that this kind of thing never happens in real life. The market, you may well argue, is efficient and things are priced at what they are worth.

Consider this: In 1988 Coca-Cola had shown a consistent capacity for earning high rates of return on shareholders' equity—in the neighborhood of 33% annually. If you had invested $100,000 in Coca-Cola stock in 1988 and held it for twelve years, till 2000, your $100,000 investment would have grown to approximately $1,100,000 in stock market value. This equates to a pretax annual compounding rate of return of approximately 22%. Let me repeat that: if you invested $100,000 in Coca-Cola stock in 1988, twelve years later you'd be worth $1,100,000. Add in the dividends that you would have received—approximately $100,080—and your pretax annual compounding rate of return goes to 23%. Think about earning a pretax annual compounding rate of return of 23% for twelve years with an investment in such a low-tech product as Coke. It's incredible!

Warren saw Coca-Cola's consumer monopoly at that time, and the high rates of return that it was earning on shareholders' equity, and bought $592.9 million worth of the stock. The rest is the stuff investment legends, and billionaires, are made of.

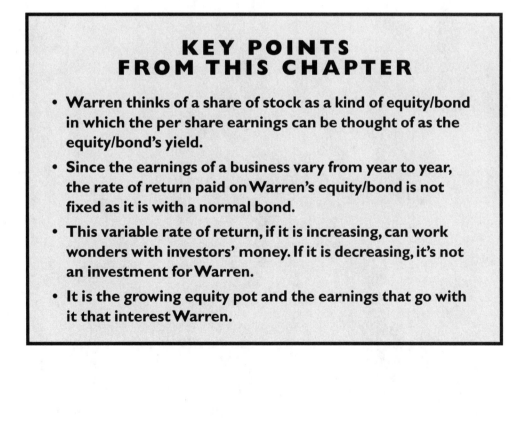

## KEY POINTS
## FROM THIS CHAPTER

- Warren thinks of a share of stock as a kind of equity/bond in which the per share earnings can be thought of as the equity/bond's yield.

- Since the earnings of a business vary from year to year, the rate of return paid on Warren's equity/bond is not fixed as it is with a normal bond.

- This variable rate of return, if it is increasing, can work wonders with investors' money. If it is decreasing, it's not an investment for Warren.

- It is the growing equity pot and the earnings that go with it that interest Warren.

## Study Questions

Why are high rates of return on shareholders' equity important?

Why is Warren uninterested in companies that have low rates of return on shareholders' equity?

What effect does a high rate of return on shareholders' equity have on the annual compounding rate of return that you will earn?

If Company A has shareholders' equity of $10 a share and earnings of $1 a share, what is its rate of return on shareholders' equity?_____

Answer: 10%

# 14: FINANCIAL CALCULATION #6: DETERMINING THE PROJECTED ANNUAL COMPOUNDING RATE OF RETURN

## PART I

Warren has figured out a way to project the annual compounding rate of return that a potential investment in one of these consumer monopolies might produce. Then when the stock price drops to a point that makes the projected annual compounding rate of return attractive, Warren buys the stock. The bad news phenomenon creates the buying situation. The projected annual compounding rate of return determines whether or not Warren pushes the button and makes the buy. Too high a stock price (which creates a low projected annual compounding rate of return) and Warren lets the purchase pass. A really low stock price (which creates a high projected annual compounding rate of return) and Warren whips out his checkbook.

In Warren's world the projected annual compounding rate of return reigns supreme. Before we delve into this formula, however, you should understand that the mathematical equations we are discussing merely serve to give you a better picture of the economic nature of the beast. As such, each of these calculations will tell you something a little different. All describe the same business, but each gives you another perspective of the business's earning power. Earning power is the key to predictability and predicting future results is the key to becoming wealthy.

Warren has defined the intrinsic value of a business as the sum of all the business's future earnings discounted to present value, using treasury bonds as the appropriate discount rate. Warren cites "The Theory of Investment Value" by John Burr Williams (Harvard University Press, 1938) as his source for this definition. Williams, on the other hand, cites Robert F. Wiese, "Investing for Future Values" (*Barron's,* Sept. 8, 1930, p. 5). Wiese stated that "The proper price of any security, whether stock or bond, is the sum of all future income payments discounted at the current rate of interest in order to arrive at the present value." (It is interesting to note that both Williams and Wiese were referring to future dividends paid out and not the future earnings of the company. Warren uses future earnings to calculate the discounted value, regardless of whether or not they are paid out as dividends.)

We all know that projecting what a business might earn over the next 100 years is next to impossible. You could try, but the realities of the world dictate that some change would occur and destroy or change the economics of the business in question. Just look at the television industry. It was hardly a bump on the economic landscape in the 1940s. In the '60s and '70s it was a fantastic business for everyone involved. After all, there were only three channels. So great was their monopoly position that Warren said in the early '80s that if he had to invest in just one company and then go away to a deserted island for ten years, it would be Capital Cities. Quite a vote of confidence.

But by the year 2000 Warren was of the opinion that the television business was not what it used to be. Dozens of channels all compete for ad revenue, and television as an industry competes with the Internet for the viewer's eye. Absolutely unsinkable businesses are hard to find.

History tells us that whether your name is Medici, Krupp, Rothschild, Winchester, or Rockefeller, the wheels of commerce may not always turn in your favor. Monopolies like those held by the early television networks can vanish almost overnight due to a change in technology or the hands of government regulators. The Medici family of Venice spent the last 500 years trying to get over the fact that the Dutch sailed around the horn of Africa and destroyed Venice's monopoly on trade with the Orient. Things change, and though the history of commerce sometimes repeats itself, fortune favors the brave and the brave constantly test the fertile waters of commerce, looking for new ways of making a buck.

Keeping this in mind, it's sheer folly to think that you have a chance in a million of projecting a company's earnings for fifty to one hundred years. There are just too many variables. It may be true in theory, but in reality, summing up all of a company's future earnings and discounting them to present value creates impossible number combinations, especially if you are factoring a constant rate of growth.

Some analysts try to solve this problem by dividing the future earnings into two different periods. The first is assigned the high growth rate and the second is assigned a lower rate. The problem here, as Williams discussed, is that any time you have a rate of earnings growth that is less than the rate of interest used in the discounting equation, the stock will end up having a finite value, even though growth continues on without limits. (See Williams, "The Theory of Investment Value," p. 89.)

An additional problem is the discount rate. If you choose treasury bonds you are in effect discounting the business's future earnings at a rate that makes them relative to the return on treasuries. Thus, if the rate of interest changes, then your valuation changes as well. The higher the interest rate, the lower the valuation. The lower the interest rate, the higher the valuation.

One other problem with using treasury bonds as a discount rate is that their yield is quoted in pretax terms. So a treasury bond that is paying a return of 8% will only earn the individual investor an after tax rate of return of 5.52%. The future earnings of the company that are being discounted are quoted in after–corporate income tax terms, which means that an 8% return will remain an 8% return unless it is paid out as a dividend.

Warren projects the per share equity value of the company in question forward for a period of ten years. This is done by using historical trends for the return on shareholders' equity less the dividend payout rate.

Warren determines the approximate shareholders' equity value of the company at the future date, in ten years, and then multiplies the per share equity value by the projected future rate of return on shareholders' equity ten years out. This gives him the projected future per share earnings of the company. Using this figure, he is then able to project a future trading value for the company's stock. Using the price he paid for the stock as the present value, he can calculate his estimated annual compounding rate of return. He then compares this projected annual compounding rate of return to what other investments, of comparable risk, are projected to pay, and what his needs are to keep ahead of inflation.

Let's look at Berkshire Hathaway. In 1986, Berkshire had stockholders' equity of $2,073 a share. For the period from 1964 to 1986, Berkshire's rate of return for stockholders' equity was 23.3% compounded annually. If you want to project the company's shareholders' equity per share figure for 2000, all you have to do is get out your trusty Texas Instruments BA-35 Solar financial calculator and switch to the financial mode and perform a future value calculation. Let's do it.

First you punch in 1986's per share equity value of $2,073 as the present value (PV key) and then the rate of growth for the interest rate, 23.3% (%i key), then the number of years, 14 (the N key). Hit the calculation key (CPT), and then the future value key (the FV key) and the calculator tells you that in 2000 Berkshire should have a per share equity value of $38,911.

You should be asking yourself this: How much money are you willing to pay in 1986 for the right to own $38,911 in shareholders' equity in 2000? First of all, you need to determine your desired rate of return. If you are like Warren, then 15% is the minimum return you are willing to take. So all you have to do is discount $38,911 to present value using 15% as the appropriate discount rate.

First, clear your calculator of the last calculation. Punch in $38,911 as the future value (FV) and then the discount rate, 15% (%i); the number of years, 14 (N); and then hit the compute button (CPT) and the present value button (PV). The calculator will tell you that in 1986 the most money you can spend on a share and expect to get a 15% annual rate of return over the next fourteen years is $5,499 a share.

A check of the local newspaper in 1986 would tell you that the market was selling a share of Berkshire's stock for around $2,700 a share that year. You think, wow, I might be able to get even a better return than the 15% I'm looking for. To check it out, punch in $2,700 for the present value (PV) and $38,911 for the future value (FV) and 14 for the number of years (N). Then hit the compute key (CPT) and the interest key (%i) and the calculator will tell you that you can expect an annual compounding rate of return of 20.9%.

By 1999 Berkshire ended up growing its per share equity value at a compounding annual rate of approximately 24%. Berkshire grew its per share equity base to approximately $37,000 in 1999.

But get this. While you were patiently waiting for the value of Berkshire to grow, the market decided it really liked Berkshire and bid the stock to a high of $81,000 and low of $50,000 a share by 1999. If you paid $2,700 for a share of Berkshire in 1986 and sold it in 1999 for $81,000 a share this would equate to a pretax annual compounding rate of return of 29.9% on your money for the thirteen-year period. (To get the rate of return you would assign $2,700 as the present value (PV) and $81,000 as the future value (FV) and 13 as the number of years (N). Then you would punch the compute key (CPT) and then the interest key (%i), which will compute the annual compounding rate of return—29.9%.) If you sold it for $50,000 a share in 1999 you would have earned a pretax annual compounding rate of return of approximately 25%.

Let's say that you paid $81,000 for a share of Berkshire Hathaway in 1999. What would your projected pretax annual compounding rate of return be if you held the stock for ten years?

We know that Berkshire has a per share equity value in 1999 of approximately $37,000 and that it has grown at an average annual compounding rate of approximately 23% a year for the last twenty-five years. Assuming this, we can project that in ten years—in the year 2009—the per share equity value for a share of Berkshire Hathaway will be $293,260.

If you paid $81,000 in 1999 for a share of Berkshire that will have a per share equity value of $293,239 in 2009, what is your annual compounding rate of return? Punch in $293,239 for the future value (FV) and $81,000 for the present value (PV) and 10 for the number of years (N). Hit the CPT key followed by the interest key (%i) and presto—your annual compounding rate of return is 13.7%. Not as interesting as 23%. Berkshire at $81,000 a share in 1999 may not be that great of a bargain from a business perspective.

Yes, the stock market may go mad by 2009 and value Berkshire considerably higher than its per share equity value—lucky you. Then again it may be valued considerably lower. But the real economic reality is that if you pay $81,000 for a share of Berkshire your annual compounding rate of return is going to be approximately 13.7%. Regardless of where the market price for the stock is short term, the long-term economics of a business will eventually dictate the stock's market price.

Remember the part of Warren's philosophy that says the price you pay determines your rate of return. Well, if you bought Berkshire at its low in 1999 of $50,000 a share and sold it for its equity value of $293,239 a share in 2009, your pretax annual compounding rate of return for the ten-year period would be 19.3%. That's far more interesting than the 13.7% you would have gotten had you paid $81,000 a share.

With Berkshire, the lower the price you pay, the higher your rate of return is going to be. The higher the price you pay, the lower the rate of return you are going to earn. Pay more, get less. Pay less, get more. It's that easy.

If you are of the opinion that Warren can't keep earning a 23% return on his capital, then you might adjust the growth rate downward to a more pedestrian 15%. With a per share equity value of approximately $37,000 in 1999, we can project that at an annual growth rate of 15% per share equity it will have increased to approximately $149,685 a share by 2009. If you paid $50,000 for a share of Berkshire in 1999 and sold it for $149,685 in the year 2009, then your annual compounding rate of return would be approximately 11.5%. Pay the high price of $81,000 a share and your annual rate of return drops to a measly 6.3%, which is not very interesting or very profitable.

You can make a stock market price adjustment to this calculation by figuring that over the last twenty-five years Berkshire has traded in the market for anywhere from approximately one to two times its per share equity value. If it trades at double its projected per share equity value in 2009, you naturally are going to do a lot better.

So let's say that you managed to pay $50,000 in 1999 for a share of Berkshire and sold it for $586,478 or double its projected 23% annual compounding equity growth per share value in 2009 of $293,239. Your projected annual pretax compounding rate of return for the ten-year period would be approximately 27.9%. This is absolutely the best-case scenario, provided you pay the cheap price of $50,000 a share. Warren keeps hitting those 23% home runs, and the stock market is lusting for Berkshire in 2009. Any hope of doing better is pie in the sky.

---

## KEY POINTS FROM THIS CHAPTER

- **It is impossible to discount the future income stream of a company that has ever-increasing net earnings.**
- **It is also impossible to determine what a company will earn over the next fifty years.**
- **It is possible to determine approximately what a company will be earning ten years from now.**
- **Pay less, earn more. Pay more, earn less.**

---

## Study Questions

Why does the return on your investment increase if you pay less?

Why is it impossible to determine what a company will earn fifty years from now?

Why is it possible to determine approximately what a company will be earning in ten years?

Why is Berkshire's future price dependent on Warren's ability to keep earnings at a high rate of return on shareholders' equity?

## Story Problems

1. If Company A has earned on average an annual return on shareholders' equity of 20% for the last ten years and it has a per share equity value of $10 in 2000 and it retains 100% of its earnings, what will its projected per

share equity value be in 2010? What will its per share earnings be in 2010?

2. Using the financial figures for Berkshire Hathaway, fill in the following example to calculate Berkshire's future stock price in 2009.

<u>Actual Year Per Share/Shareholders' Equity</u>

| | | | | |
|---|---|---|---|---|
| 1. | **1999** | | <u>$37,000</u> → | **Present Value (base year)** |
| 2. | **2000** | **one** | _____ | Financial calculation for use with TI BA-35 |
| 3. | **2001** | **two** | _____ | Solar Calculator: **Future trading price** |
| 4. | **2002** | **three** | _____ | **of Berkshire.** Use 1999's shareholders' |
| 5. | **2003** | **four** | _____ | equity as your present value (PV) and 23% |
| 6. | **2004** | **five** | _____ | as your interest rate (%i) and 10 as your |
| 7. | **2005** | **six** | _____ | number of years (N). Hit the compute key |
| 8. | **2006** | **seven** | _____ | (CPT) and then the future value key (FV). |
| 9. | **2007** | **eight** | _____ | This computes the future value of share |
| 10. | **2008** | **nine** | _____ | holders' equity for Berkshire in 2009. |
| 11. | **2009** | **ten** | _____ → | **Future value** |

↑

**Number of Years**          **Berkshire's projected shareholders'**
**from Base Year**            **equity in 2009 _____.**

(Note: If you feel inspired, calculate Berkshires' shareholders' equity for all the projected years and then calculate the future trading price for those years as well.)

Answers: 1. $61.91 per share equity value. $12.38 per share earnings.
2. The projected shareholders' equity per share for Berkshire in 2009 is $293,260.

# 15: DETERMINING THE PROJECTED ANNUAL COMPOUNDING RATE OF RETURN

## PART II

In the preceding chapter we learned how to *calculate the future value of Berkshire Hathaway by projecting its future per share equity value. We also saw that once a future value is determined it is possible to project the annual compounding rate of return the investment will earn.*

In this chapter we will project the future per share earnings of a company and then determine its future market price. We will then use the results of these calculations to project the annual compounding rate of return that the investment in question will produce.

Let's examine at this point an actual example of Warren's decision making, namely, the financial reasoning that led Warren to take his initial position in Coca-Cola. (Please note: All the historical figures given for Coca-Cola have been adjusted to reflect stock splits through 2000.)

### The Coca-Cola Company—1988

In 1988, Warren, using his equity as a bond rationale, had his holding company, Berkshire Hathaway, buy 113,380,000 Coca-Cola equity/bonds (stock) at $5.22 a share, for a total investment of $592,540,000. In 1988, Coca-Cola had shareholders' equity of $1.07 a share and net earnings of $0.36 a share. From Warren's point of view, each Coca-Cola equity/bond that he had just bought had a coupon attached to it that paid $0.36. This means that each of Warren's equity/bond shares was yielding 33.6% return on shareholders' equity ($.36 ÷ $1.07 = 33.6%), of which approximately 58% was retained by the company and 42% was to be paid out as a dividend to the shareholders.

Thus, in theory, when Warren bought his Coca-Cola equity/bond share with a per share equity value of $1.07, he calculated that his $1.07 equity/bond would effectively earn a 33.6% return. He also figured that this 33.6% return was divided into two different types of yields.

One yield would represent 58% of the 33.6% return on shareholders' equity and would be retained by the company. This amount is equal to $0.21 of the $0.36 in per share earnings. This portion of the yield is the after–corporate tax portion and is subject to no more state or federal taxes.

The other yield is the remaining 42% of the 33.6% return on shareholders' equity, which is paid out as a dividend. This amount is equal to $0.15 of the $0.36 per share earnings. This portion of the return is subject to personal or corporate taxes for dividends.

So our 33.6% return on shareholders' equity is two different yields. One is a 19.4% return on shareholders' equity equal to $0.21, which is retained by the Coca-Cola Company and added to Coca-Cola's shareholders' equity base.

The other is a 14.2% return on shareholders' equity equal to $0.15, which is paid out to the shareholders of Coca-Cola as a dividend.

## TABLE A Year—1988

Coca-Cola's $1.07 (per share equity value × .336 (return on equity) = $0.36 a share in earnings.

The $0.36 is divided into two portions. One portion is retained by the company and is equal to 58% of the per share earnings or $0.21. The other portion is paid out as a dividend to the shareholders and is equal to 42% of the per share earnings, or $0.15.

$0.21 retained to shareholders' equity
AND
$0.15 paid out as a dividend

If we assume that Coca-Cola can maintain this 33.6% return on shareholders' equity for the next twelve years and continues to retain 58% of this return and pay out as a dividend the other 4%, then it is possible to project the company's future per share equity value and its per share earnings.

This is done by taking 58% of the 33.6% return on shareholders' equity, or 19.4%, and adding it to the per share equity base each year.

So, if in 1988 Coca-Cola had a per share equity value of $1.07, we would increase the $1.07 by 19.4%, to give us a projected per share equity value for 1989 of $1.27 ($1.07 × 1.194 = $1.27)

You can calculate this with your Texas Instruments BA-35 Solar calculator by punching in $1.07 as the present value (PV) and 19.4 as the compounding rate of interest (i%) and 1 for the number of years (N). Then hit the CPT key and the punch the future value key (FV). This will give you a per share future value of $1.27 for 1989.

If you want to know *what the per share equity value will be in 1998,* all you have to do is punch in $1.07 for the present value (PV) and 19.4 as the compounding rate of growth (i%) and 10 for the number of years (N). Then hit the CPT and push the future value key (FV) and this will give you a projected per share equity value of $6.30 for 1998.

*If you want to project the per share earnings,* all you have to do is multiply the per share equity value by 33.6%. In the case of 1989 we would multiply per share equity value of $1.27 by 33.6% and get projected per share earnings of $0.42. To do this for the year 1998 we would multiply the projected per share equity of $6.30 by 33.6% and get projected per share earnings of $2.11.

Let's do the calculations and project out the per share equity value and per share earnings of Coca-Cola for twelve years beginning in 1988 and ending in 2000.

### Projections for 1988 to 2000
### Table AA

| Year | Equity Value | Per Share Earnings | Dividends Paid Out | Retained Earnings |
|------|--------------|--------------------|--------------------|-------------------|
| 1988 | $1.07 | $0.36 | $0.15 | $0.21 |
| 1989 | $1.28 | $0.43 | $0.18 | $0.25 |
| 1990 | $1.53 | $0.51 | $0.21 | $0.30 |
| 1991 | $1.83 | $0.61 | $0.26 | $0.35 |
| 1992 | $2.18 | $0.72 | $0.30 | $0.42 |
| 1993 | $2.60 | $0.87 | $0.37 | $0.50 |
| 1994 | $3.10 | $1.04 | $0.44 | $0.60 |
| 1995 | $3.70 | $1.24 | $0.52 | $0.72 |
| 1996 | $4.42 | $1.48 | $0.62 | $0.86 |
| 1997 | $5.28 | $1.77 | $0.75 | $1.02 |
| 1998 | $6.30 | $2.12 | $0.90 | $1.22 |
| 1999 | $7.52 | $2.53 | $1.07 | $1.46 |
| 2000 | $8.98 | $3.02 | $1.27 | $1.75 |
| | | | TOTAL: $7.04 | $9.66 |

Projections usually aren't worth the paper they are written on. Most financial analysts are only willing to project earnings for a year or two in advance and then they give you an overview of the company and pronounce it a buy. But Graham felt that the real role of the analyst was to ascertain the earning power of the business and make a long-term projection of what the company was capable of earning.

In table AA we have projected per share earnings out for twelve years. In most situations this would be an act of insanity. However, as Warren discovered, if the company is one of sufficient earning power and earns high rates of return on shareholders' equity (created by a consumer monopoly), chances are good that fairly accurate long-term projections of earnings can be made.

From a 1989 perspective, if Coca-Cola can maintain a 33.6% return on shareholders' equity in the twelve years from 1988 to 2000, we can project that the company will be earning approximately $3.02 a share in 2000. By 2000 Warren will also have earned an after-tax pool of dividend payouts equal to $686 million (dividend pool of $7.04 × 113.38 million shares, minus income tax on dividends of approximately 14% = $686 million).

So Warren can also project that by 2000 his investment in Coca-Cola will have paid back his original investment of $592,401,000 and he still gets to keep the 113.38 million shares of Coca-Cola stock as profit. If the company is trading at a historically conservative rate of fifteen times our projected earnings of $3.02 a share, then the 113.38 million shares of the Coca-Cola stock should be worth $45.30 a share (15 × 3.02 = $45.30) or $5.136 billion ($45.30 × 113.38 million shares = $5.136 billion). Not bad for a day's work.

- **Please note: When you are choosing a price to earnings ratio (P/E) by which to multiply your projected future per share earnings, you get the best perspective by running your calculations with the average annual P/E ratio for the last ten years. You should also run your equations with the high and the low P/E ratio for the last ten years, just to give you a better perspective of how well you might or might not do. But BE WARNED: stocks don't always trade at their historically high P/E. Using a historically high P/E ratio can create disastrously inaccurate projections! Stick with the average annual P/E ratio for the last ten years, especially if there has been a huge spread between the high and the low P/E ratio within the last ten years. When in doubt, choose the middle road. (Note: The Value Line Investment Survey lists the average annual P/E for ten to fifteen years back.)**

If we are projecting per share earnings of $3.02 for Coca-Cola in 2000, we can estimate that the market price for the stock will range from fifteen to twenty-five times per share earnings. (This equates to a P/E ratio between 15 and 25.) This means that the stock is projected to be trading in a price range of between $45.30 (15 × $3.02 = $45.30) and $75.50 a share (25 × $3.02 = $75.50) in 2000. We also know that Warren's initial investment was $5.22 a share.

To determine the annual compounding rate of return for the period from 1988 to 2000, all we have to do is take out the Texas Instruments calculator and punch in 12 for the number of years (N) and $5.22 for the present value (PV) and either $45.30 or $75.50 for the future value (FV). Then hit the CPT key and the interest key (i%). This will give you the annual compounding rate of return, which in this case will equal to either 19.7% for a per share market price of $45.30, or 24.9% for a per share market price of $75.50. Thus, Warren could project an annual compounding rate of return between 19.7% and 24.9% for the twelve-year period from 1988 to 2000.

| | Year | | Stock Price | |
|---|---|---|---|---|
| 1. | 1988 | | $5.22 → | **Present value (base year)** |
| 2. | 1989 | one | ____ | Computing the **Projected Annual** |
| 3. | 1990 | two | ____ | **Compounding Rate of Return** for Warren's |
| 4. | 1991 | three | ____ | investment in Coca-Cola. Use 1988 market |
| 5. | 1992 | four | ____ | price of $5.22 for the present value (PV); 2000 |
| 6. | 1993 | five | ____ | projected values of either $45.79 or $75.00 as |
| 7. | 1994 | six | ____ | the future value (FV), 12 for the number of |
| 8. | 1995 | seven | ____ | years (N). Hit the (CPT) key and then the |
| 9. | 1996 | eight | ____ | interest key (%i) and the projected annual |
| 10. | 1997 | nine | ____ | compounding rate of return will be calculated. |
| 11. | 1998 | ten | ____ | **Projected annual compounding** |
| 12. | 1999 | eleven | ____ | **rate of return** _____. |
| 13. | 2000 | twelve | $45.79 or $75.00 → | **Future value** |

↑

**Number of Years Out from Base Year**

We can adjust these numbers to reflect the dividends that Coca-Cola paid out and any taxes Warren would have to pay if he sold the stock in 2000. To do this, take the $45.30 and subtract the amount Warren has invested in the stock, $5.22 (which is not taxed). This will give you $40.08, the amount of Warren's profit. You then subtract 35% for corporate taxes on the gain, which leaves you with $26.05. Then add in the after-tax pool of Coca-Cola dividends that Warren has been collecting for the twelve years, $6.05 ($7.04 - (14% tax) = $6.05). This gives you an after-tax profit of $32.10 ($6.05 + $26.05 = $32.10). You then add back the $5.22, for an after-tax total proceeds from the sale of $37.32 ($32.10 + $5.22 = $37.32).

With a cost basis of $5.22 a share and total after-tax sale proceeds of $37.32, total after-tax profit from the sale will be $32.10. This equates to an after-tax annual compounding rate of return of 17.8%. Thus, in 2000, if Coca-Cola is trading at fifteen times earnings and Warren elects to sell his stock, his annual compounding rate of return after taxes will be 17.8% for the twelve years from 1988 to 2000.

You can run the same sequence of calculations for a P/E of 25, which equates to a market price of $75.50 a share in 2000. After you take out taxes and add in the after-tax dividend pool, you end up with a total return of $51.73, which equates to an annual compounding rate of return of 22% for the twelve-year period. (Note: Even if Coca-Cola's stock is trading at only nine times earnings, Warren still can project an after-tax annual compounding rate of return of 14.4%.)

Imagine if we came to you and said that we wanted to sell to you, at par value, a noncallable twelve-year Coca-Cola bond that paid a tax-free, fixed annual rate of return of 14.4% or, better yet, 17.8%. How about 22%? Mouth starting to water? What would you do? We'd mortgage the farm, house, and kids and buy all we could.

However, back in 1988, you could have bought the stock in the Coca-Cola company and essentially gotten an after-tax annual compounding rate of return between 14.4% and 22%—provided that you were willing to hold the investment for a period of twelve years. (Note: As luck would have it, the stock market started valuing Coca-Cola stock in 1996 at historically high price to earnings ratios of 40 and better. This has enabled Warren to show a higher than expected annual compounding rate of return than is projected here for the period between 1988 and 2000. Be warned that using Coca-Cola's historically high P/E ratio of 40 as a current multiplier may be a bit too optimistic. *Use that average annual P/E ratio for the last ten years instead.*)

What creates all this wealth is Coca-Cola's ability to take its retained earnings and earn a 33.6% rate of return shareholders' equity. Then it can retain 58% of that 33.6%, free of personal income taxes, which is added to the shareholders' equity base in the company. This effectively compounds the retained earnings by adding them to the base sum from which they were created.

Now that we have projected Coca-Cola's per share earnings from 1988 to 2000, we can find out whether our analysis has any validity. To do this we can compare the projected per share earnings for 1988 to 1999 against the actual results reported by Coca-Cola for 1988 to 1999.

## COCA-COLA COMPARISON OF PER SHARE EARNINGS PROJECTIONS TO ACTUAL RESULTS

| Year | Projected Earnings | Actual Earnings | Margin of Error |
|------|--------------------|-----------------|-----------------|
| 1. 1989 | $0.43 | $0.42 | 2.3% |
| 2. 1990 | $0.51 | $0.51 | 0% |
| 3. 1991 | $0.61 | $0.61 | 0% |
| 4. 1992 | $0.72 | $0.72 | 0% |
| 5. 1993 | $0.87 | $0.84 | 3.5% |
| 6. 1994 | $1.04 | $0.99 | 5% |
| 7. 1995 | $1.24 | $1.19 | 4% |
| 8. 1996 | $1.48 | $1.40 | 5.4% |
| 9. 1997 | $1.77 | $1.63 | 7.8% |
| 10. 1998 | $2.12 | $1.43 | 32.5% |
| 11. 1999 | $2.43 | $0.98 | 59.5% → Problem year for Coke |

We can see that our margin for error is running between 0% and 7.8% on projections running from 1989 forward for nine years. Not too bad. But as you can see in '98 and '99 the margin for error becomes greater. What we couldn't see back in 1988 was that Coca-Cola would experience three events that would hurt profits in those years. The first was a broad recession that swept through Asia (remember: even a strong consumer monopoly can fall prey to the business cycle). The second was a Coca-Cola bottling plant in Belgium that inadvertently served up a tainted batch of soda that made a few people ill. This led to expensive recalls of the product in Belgium and France and tarnished Coke's reputation for delivering a quality product. The third was a costly program of corporate restructuring designed to increase Coke's long-term profitability. As you might remember, these "bad news" kinds of events usually result in a drop in the company's share price. That is exactly what happened, Coke's stock price tumbled from a high in 1999 of $70 a share to $52 a share in 2000.

We projected in 1988 that in 2000 Coke would be trading between $45 and $75 a share, and it was. Coke's stock price rose to this level even with all the bad press. This makes the 113.38 million shares that Warren bought in 1988 worth $6.235 billion, which equates to a pretax annual compounding rate of return of 21.6% on his original investment for the twelve-year period between 1988 and 2000. What happened? The stock market became aware of the long-term power of Coke's economic engine and bid the stock price up to a P/E ratio of between 40 and 50. Things don't always work exactly the way one plans, but if you have a consumer monopoly as strong as Coke has, the surprise is usually on the upside. In Warren's case the upside surprise was worth a $5.6 billion profit on his original investment of $592 million.

A British investment saying goes: "Lots of ups and just a few downs can still fill your pocket with millions of pounds." Coca-Cola may suffer a few bumps, but in the end the power of its economic engine will continue to make its shareholders rich. Things do go better with Coke, including your money.

---

## KEY POINTS FROM THIS CHAPTER

- **It is possible to predict with a fair degree of accuracy the future earnings of some companies, and in so doing, to draw a fairly accurate picture of what the stock trading price will be ten years out.**

- **When projecting a future stock price based on an earnings projection, always use the average P/E ratio for the last ten years.**

- **The power of Coke's consumer monopoly is sufficient to overcome the vicissitudes of most business problems that it will face in the foreseeable future.**

---

## Study Questions

Why was Coke able to suffer business problems that resulted in a severe decline in earnings yet still meet Warren's price projection for the stock in 2000?

Why does the stock market value a consumer monopoly so highly?

# 16: FINANCIAL CALCULATION #7: THE EQUITY/BOND WITH AN EXPANDING COUPON

Warren has more than one way of looking at an investment situation. One is to view a stock as an equity/bond with an expanding coupon. You might be wondering where the coupon concept comes from. Bonds used to come with dozens of *coupons* attached to them. You'd clip a coupon and send it to the company that issued the bond and it would send you the fixed rate of interest that the bond had earned for a particular period of time. That way the company didn't have to keep track of who owned the bond. Today bonds are *registered* with the company that issued them and a bond holder gets the interest checks in the mail without clipping or mailing anything. In Warren's world the equity/bonds of certain companies have a coupon that is increasing. Each year the equity/bond pays the holder a little more. Thus, the equity/bond with an expanding coupon.

Let's see how this works with the Coca-Cola situation. Remember what we said earlier: What you pay for a stock determines your rate of return. When Warren purchased his initial interest in Coca-Cola in 1988, the company had shareholders' equity of $1.07 a share and earnings of $0.36 a share. This amounts to a 33.6% return on shareholders' equity. If you paid $1.07 for a share of Coca-Cola, you would be buying it at its per share equity value of $1.07, which would give you an initial rate of return of 33.6% ($0.36 ÷ $1.07 = 33.6%). However, Warren didn't pay $1.07 a share, he paid approximately $5.22 a share, which means that his rate of return on his Coca-Cola equity/bond would be approximately 6.89% ($0.36 ÷ $5.22 = 6.89%) or well below the 33.6% that Coca-Cola was earning on its shareholders' equity base in 1988.

An initial rate of return of 6.89% is not all that great. But Warren was projecting that Coca-Cola's per share earnings would continue to grow and in the process cause an annual increase in his rate of return. Sound enticing? Let's look closer.

We can explain Coca-Cola's economics from several vantage points, but the key is the return on shareholders' equity and retained earnings. In 1988 Warren earns $0.36 a share on his original investment of $5.22, which equates to a 6.89% rate of return. If it *retains* approximately 58% of that $0.36, or $0.21 ($0.36 × .58 = $0.21), Coca-Cola will have effectively reinvested $0.21 of Warren's money back into the company. (Note: The other 42% of the $0.36, or $0.15, is paid out as a dividend.)

So in the beginning of 1989, Warren will have invested in his Coca-Cola stock his original 1988 investment of $5.22 a share, plus 1988's retained earnings of $0.21 a share, for a total investment of $5.43 a share ($5.22 + $0.21 = $5.43).

At the beginning of 1989, Warren's total investment in Coca-Cola is projected to be:

| | |
|---|---|
| Original 1988 Investment | $5.22 |
| Retained Earnings for 1988 | $0.21 |
| 1989 Total Per Share Investment | $5.43 |

We can project that in 1989 the original $5.22 portion of the $5.43 that Warren now has invested in Coca-Cola stock will still earn $0.36 or 6.89%. If Coca-Cola can maintain a 33.6% return on shareholders' equity, we can project that in 1989 the $0.21 of retained earnings from 1988 will earn a rate of return of 33.6%. So $0.21 a share in retained earnings will produce $0.07 a share in new earnings in 1989 ($0.21 × 33.6% = $0.07). This means that projected 1989 earnings will be **$0.43** a share ($0.36 + $0.07 = $0.43).

Warren will be earning 6.89% or $0.36 on his original 1988 investment of $5.22 a share and a return of 33.6% or $0.07 a share on retained earnings of $0.21 a share. This means that in 1989 his Coca-Cola stock earns $0.43 a share, which gives him a 7.9% rate of return on his initial investment plus retained earnings of $5.43 a share ($0.43 ÷ $5.43 = 7.9%).

## PROJECTED PER SHARE RETURN ON INVESTED AND RETAINED CAPITAL FOR 1989

| | |
|---|---|
| Original 1988 Investment | $5.22 × 6.89% = $0.36 |
| Retained Earnings for 1988 | +$0.21 × 33.6% = $0.07 |
| 1989 Total Per Share Investment | $5.43   Earnings Per Share $0.43 |

Rate of return on total capital invested for 1989: Earnings per share of $0.43 ÷ Invested and Retained Capital of $5.43 = 7.9% Rate of Return.

The same analysis can be run for 1990 as well. Coca-Cola will retain 58% of the $0.43 per share earnings from 1989, or approximately $0.25. This will add $0.25 to the $5.43 that Warren already has invested in Coca-Cola. So his investment in Coca-Cola stock at the beginning of 1990 will be the original 1988 investment of $5.22, plus the retained earnings from 1988, $0.21, plus the retained earnings from 1989, $0.25, for a total of $5.68 ($5.22 + $0.21 + $0.25 = $5.68).

## TOTAL PER SHARE INVESTMENT IN COCA-COLA AT THE BEGINNING OF 1990

| | |
|---|---|
| Original 1988 Investment | $5.22 |
| Retained Earnings '88 & '89 | +$0.46 |
| 1990 Total Per Share Investment | $5.68 |

We can project that in 1990, Warren's original investment of $5.22 a share will earn 6.89% or $0.36 a share. But the retained earnings from 1988 ($0.21 a share) and from 1989 ($0.25 a share) *will each earn the current rate of return on shareholders' equity, which is projected to be 33.6%.* This $0.46 a share ($0.21 + $0.25 = $0.46) in retained earnings from '88 and '89 will produce earnings of $0.15 a share in 1990 ($0.46 × 33.6% = $0.15). Thus total earnings for 1990 are projected to be $0.51 a share ($0.36 + $0.15 = $0.51). This means that in 1990 Warren's projected rate of return on invested and retained capital of $5.68 a share will be $0.51 a share. This equates to an 8.9% rate of return on his initial investment plus retained earnings from 1988 and 1989 ($0.51 ÷ $5.68 = 8.9%).

## PROJECTED PER SHARE RETURN ON INVESTED AND RETAINED CAPITAL FOR 1990

| | |
|---|---|
| Original 1988 Investment | $5.22 × 6.89% = $0.36 |
| Retained Earnings for '88 and '89 | $0.46 × 33.6% = $0.15 |
| 1990 Total Per Share Investment | $5.68 Earnings Per Share $0.41 |

Rate of return on total capital invested for 1989: Earnings Per Share $0.51 ÷ Invested and Retained Capital of $5.68 = 8.9% Rate of Return.

We're sure you noticed the increasing rate of return, but what we really want you to see here is that Warren's original investment in Coca-Cola is fixed at a rate of return of 6.89%, but the retained earnings are free to earn the full 33.6%. Think of it as if you bought a Coca-Cola equity/bond that paid a return of 6.89% and every time you got an interest check in the mail you could reinvest it in a new Coca-Cola equity/bond that would pay a 33.6% annual compounding rate of return. The only catch to getting the 33.6% annual compounding rate of return is that you have to first buy the Coca-Cola equity/bond paying 6.89%.

You pay a steep price to get in the door, but once you get in, it's heaven. And the longer you stay, the better it gets.

---

## KEY POINTS FROM THIS CHAPTER

- **Warren views a stock as an equity/bond with an expanding coupon.**
- **The initial rate of return is determined by the price you pay for the stock, and the return on retained earnings is determined by the rate of return on shareholders' equity.**
- **You sometimes pay a steep price to get in the door but after that you earn what the company earns on its shareholders' equity base.**

---

## Study Questions

Why does Warren view a share of stock as an equity/bond with an expanding coupon?

Why is the coupon on Warren's equity/bond expanding?

# 17: FINANCIAL CALCULATION #8: USING THE PER SHARE EARNINGS ANNUAL GROWTH RATE TO PROJECT AN INVESTMENT'S COMPOUNDING ANNUAL RATE OF RETURN

It is possible to project the future price of a company's stock by using the company's per share earnings annual growth rate. First we project a future year's per share earnings and then project the stock's price. If we know the stock's future price, the price we paid for it, and the number of years the investment is held, then we can project the annual compounding rate of return the investment will give us.

Here we will use Capital Cities as an example. Capital Cities had very consistent per share earnings growth for the ten-year period from 1970 to 1980. We will project per share earnings from 1980 ten years forward to 1990. Then we will project a price range that Capital Cities stock will be trading at in 1990. Finally, we'll determine the annual compounding rate of return you would have earned if you had bought a share of Capital Cities in 1980 and sold it in 1990.

## To Project Capital Cities' Future Per Share Earnings for 1990

From 1970 to 1980, Capital Cities per share net income grew from $0.08 to $0.53, or at an annual compounding rate of approximately 20%. If we projected the per share earnings of Capital Cities forward ten years from 1980, to the year 1990, using a 20% rate of growth, we would get projected per share earnings of $3.28 for 1990. The equation for this is PV = $0.53, N = 10, %i = 20%, punch the CPT button and then the future value (FV) button and you get a calculated $3.28. So in 1990 Capital Cities will have per share earnings of $3.28.

### To Project the Market Price of Capital Cities Stock in 1990

A review of the price/earnings ratio for Capital Cities for the period of 1970 to 1980 indicates that the stock traded at anywhere from nine to twenty-five times earnings. Let's say for argument's sake that we are as conservative as old Ronald Reagan—we'll use the low end of the P/E range, nine times earnings for our calculations. Thus our projected 1990 earnings of $3.28 a share equates to a projected 1990 market price for the stock of $29.52 ($3.28 × 9 = $29.52).

### To Project the Annual Compounding Rate of Return You Would Have Earned if You Had Bought a Share of Capital Cities in 1980 and Sold It in 1990

By looking in *The Wall Street Journal*, you can see that Capital Cities stock in 1980 commonly traded for around $5 a share. Get out your Texas Instruments BA-35 Solar calculator and punch in PV = $5, FV = $29.52, number of years N = 10, and hit the CPT key. Then hit the interest key, %i, and you get an annual compounding rate of return of 19.4%. This means that if you spent $5 a share for Capital Cities stock in 1980, you could have projected an expected annual compounding rate of return of 19.4% for the next ten years.

Now let's see what really would have happened to the $5 a share investment made in 1980. In 1990 the company had earnings of $2.77 a share compared to our estimate of $3.28 a share. (Okay, it's not an exact science.) The stock in 1990 traded in a price range of between $38 and $63 a share compared to our estimate of $29.52 a share. Let's say you sold your stock at $38 a share in 1990. Your annual compounding rate of return on the $5 investment you made in 1980 would be (PV = $5, FV = $38, N = 10; hit the CPT key and %i key and you get 22.4%). So your pretax annual compounding rate of return would have been 22.4% for the ten-year period between 1980 and 1990. If you had sold it in 1990 for the high price of $63 a share, your pretax annual compounding rate of return would have been 28.8% for the ten-year period between 1980 and 1990.

Thus, in the case of Capital Cities, the stock market revalued the stock to a higher price multiple than we projected and in the process increased our fortunes above our expectations.

(In case you are wondering, if you had invested **$100,000** in Capital Cities at $5 a share, back in 1980, it would have compounded annually at 22.4% and grown to be worth approximately **$754,769.21** by 1990.)

You should understand that Warren is not calculating a specific value for the stock, as many Warren watchers and writers believe. Warren is not saying that Capital Cities is worth X per share and I can buy it for half of X, as Graham used to do. Warren is instead asking, if I pay X per share for Capital Cities stock, given the economic realities for the company, what is my expected annual compounding rate of return going to be at the end of ten years? After determining the expected annual compounding rate of return, Warren then compares it to other investments and the annual compounding rate of return that he needs to stay ahead of inflation.

By functioning in this manner he can buy a stock and not care whether he ever sees where Wall Street is valuing it. Warren knows approximately what his long-term annual compounding rate of return is going to be. He also knows that over the long term the market will value the company to reflect this increase in the company's net worth.

If Warren bought from the Graham point of view—that a share of a company was worth $10, and Warren was able to buy it for $5 a share, he would sell when the stock market valued the company at $10 a share—then Warren would have to have his nose glued to *The Wall Street Journal* every day to see where the market was valuing the stock. That's not his way.

## KEY POINTS FROM THIS CHAPTER

- **If the company has a consumer monopoly, it is possible to project the future price of the company's stock by using the company's per share annual growth rate.**

- **Warren is not calculating a specific value for a stock.**

- **Warren asks himself this question: If I pay X for a share of stock, given the economic realities of the business, what is my expected annual compounding rate of return going to be in ten years?**

- **Warren compares his projections to what other investments are paying.**

- **By functioning in this manner Warren can buy a stock and never care whether he gets a daily quote on where Wall Street is valuing it.**

## Study Questions

Why doesn't Warren calculate a specific value for a stock?

Why does Warren compare investment returns?

Why doesn't Warren care what Wall Street thinks his investments are worth on a day-to-day basis?

## 18: FINANCIAL CALCULATION #9: WHY WARREN LOVES STOCK REPURCHASE PROGRAMS OR HOW CAN A COMPANY INCREASE ITS SHARE-HOLDERS' FORTUNES BY BUYING BACK THE COMPANY'S STOCK

Once Warren has made an investment in one of these wonderful consumer monopoly type businesses, he lobbies the company's board of directors to begin a share repurchase program. He does this because he has figured out that when a business in which he owns an interest repurchases its own shares, it is effectively shrinking the number of shares outstanding, which in turn increases Warren's ownership interest in the company without Warren's having to invest another penny.

Here is how it works. Let's say that a company has 100 million shares outstanding and Warren owns 10 million of those shares, which equates to owning 10% of the entire business. If the company over the next year goes into the stock market and buys back 40 million of its shares, it will have only 60 million shares outstanding. Warren's ownership interest in the business would have increased from 10% to 16.6%. His ownership in the company increased without investing any more money. The company's own capital was used to increase his ownership interest.

Now consider this: If the company had paid out the money that it spent on buying back its shares, Warren would have had to pay income tax on his portion of the dividend disbursement, which means that he would have had about 30% less money to invest with. By having the company repurchase its own shares, Warren is able to avoid the tax man and in the process increase his percentage of ownership in the business. Let's take a closer look.

When Berkshire Hathaway bought into *The Washington Post,* it acquired approximately 10% of the *Post* for $10.2 million. Today Berkshire owns approximately 17.2% of the company. Berkshire's increase in ownership from

10% to 17.2% was a direct result of *The Washington Post*'s stock repurchase program, which Warren helped instigate shortly after he joined the *Post's* board of directors. Today *The Washington Post* has 10.04 million shares outstanding and is trading at approximately $500 a share. This equates to a market capitalization of $5.02 billion (10.04 million × $500 = $5.02 billion). If *The Washington Post* hadn't engaged in repurchasing its own shares, then Berkshire's interest in the company would still be 10%—which today would be worth approximately $502 million ($5.02 billion × .10 = $502 million). But since *The Washington Post* did repurchase its shares, Berkshire now owns 17.2% of the company—which today is worth approximately $863.4 million ($5.02 billion × 0.172 = $863.4 million). Because of *The Washington Post*'s share repurchase program, Berkshire was able to see a $334.4 million increase in its net worth that would not have occurred if there hadn't been a share repurchase program ($863.4 million – $502 million = $334.4 million).

Warren did the same kind of thing with Berkshire's 1980 initial investment in Geico. He acquired 33% of all its outstanding shares for $45.7 million. By 1995, Geico's share repurchase program had increased Berkshire's stake in Geico to approximately 50%. In 1995 Geico had a total market capitalization of approximately $4.7 billion. If Berkshire had still owned only 33% of Geico in 1995, then the total value of its 33% stake would be approximately $1.55 billion. But because of Geico's stock repurchase program, Berkshire's ownership stake in Geico increased to 50%, which in 1995 was worth $2.35 billion. This means that Geico's share repurchase program added approximately $800 million in value to Berkshire's net worth. (In 1996 Berkshire acquired the other 50% of Geico, to take control of 100% of the business.)

With share repurchases Warren has figured out how to secure a larger ownership interest in a company without making any further investment in it. A neat trick, isn't it?

## The Economics of Expending a Company's Shareholders' Equity Base on Share Repurchases

If you compare our projected per share equity value for the Coca-Cola Company from 1988 to 1993 (see page 128) with the actual per share equity values reported by Coca-Cola, you will find the following:

| Year | Projected Per Share Equity Value | Actual Per Share Equity Value |
|------|----------------------------------|-------------------------------|
| 1989 | $1.28 | $1.18 |
| 1990 | $1.53 | $1.41 |
| 1991 | $1.53 | $1.67 |
| 1992 | $2.18 | $1.49 |
| 1993 | $2.60 | $1.77 |

You can clearly see the discrepancy between our projected per share equity values and the actual reported values. What is going on here? The answer is that the Coca-Cola Company has been expending its shareholders' equity base on *retiring* its common stock. In fact, from 1984 to the end of 1993, Coca-Cola expended approximately $5.8 billion of its shareholders' equity buying back its common stock, shrinking the number of its outstanding common shares from approximately 3,174,000,000 in 1984, to approximately 2,604,000,000 by the end of 1993. This represents a reduction of approximately 570 million common shares, or 21% of all the common stock the company had outstanding in 1984.

If one considers that Coca-Cola had 3,174,000,000 outstanding shares in 1984 and that Coca-Cola spent $5.8 billion dollars of its shareholder's money over the next nine years on share repurchases, one could can argue that Coca-Cola spent approximately $1.82 a share of its shareholders' money buying back its own shares ($5.8 billion ÷ 3.174 billion shares outstanding in 1984 = $1.82 a share).

In 1993 Coca-Cola posted total net income of approximately $2,176,000,000. If you divide the total net income for 1993 by the total number of common shares outstanding at the end of 1993 (2,604,000,000 shares), you get an earnings per share figure of $0.84. (Total 1993 net income of $2,176,000,000 ÷ 2,604,000,000 outstanding shares = $0.84 a share.)

Now consider this: If at the end of 1993 there had been as many shares outstanding as there were in 1984, approximately 3,174,000,000, and Coca-Cola's 1993 total net income was $2,176,000,000, then Coca-Cola would have reported per share income for that year of $0.68. (Total 1993 net income of $2,176,000,000 ÷ 3,174,000,000 outstanding shares = $0.68 a share.)

This means that the $1.82 a share in shareholders' equity that Coca-Cola spent buying back its shares from 1984 to 1993 caused in 1993 a per share earnings increase of $0.16 (EPS in 1993 with share repurchases, $0.84, minus EPS in 1993 without share repurchases, $0.68 = $0.16 increase in per share net income).

Coca-Cola, based on 3.174 billion shares outstanding in 1983, spent approximately $1.82 a share to cause a per share earnings increase of $0.16. This equates to an approximate rate of return of 8.7% ($0.16 ÷ $1.82 = 8.7%). It may not sound all that rewarding at first but what seems to be a marginal allocation of capital on Coca-Cola's part is actually economic brilliance when you consider how the stock market interprets this $0.16 per share increase in earnings.

In 1993, the stock market valued Coca-Cola's stock at twenty-five times per share earnings. So a $0.16 increase in the per share earnings caused a $4.00 increase in market value of the stock. Let us show you how this works:

**In 1993 without Share Repurchases:** 1993 total net earnings of $2,176,000,000 ÷ 3,174,000,000 shares = per share earnings of $0.68 in 1993. If you multiply $0.68 by a P/E of 25 you get a **per share market price of $17.00** ($0.68 × 25 = $17.00).

**In 1993 with Share Repurchases:** 1993 total net earnings of $2,176,000,000 ÷ 2,604,000,000 shares = per share earnings of **$0.84 in 1993.** If you multiply $0.84 by a P/E of 25 you get a **per share market price of $21.00** ($0.84 × 25 = $21.00).

The difference between the two is **$4.00** ($21.00 - $17.00 = $4.00).

Remember that Coca-Cola spent only $1.87 a share of shareholders' money in the repurchase of its stock. Thus, the $1.87 a share of shareholders' money spent produced a $4.00 increase in Coca-Cola's per share market price. By spending its shareholders' equity base to retire its common stock Coca-Cola effectively shrank both its shareholders' equity base and the number of its outstanding shares. Though this doesn't change total net earnings, it does increase per share earnings because the number of shares have decreased. The pie remains the same size. The pieces have just gotten bigger.

Also, since the shareholders' equity base has decreased, the return on shareholders' equity will increase as well. (Remember, the return on shareholders' equity is determined by dividing the net earnings by the shareholders' equity value. You can increase the rate of return on shareholders' equity by increasing the net earnings or by decreasing the amount of shareholders' equity in the company.)

The bottom line here is that Coca-Cola spent $1.87 a share of its shareholders' money to repurchase its stock, which caused per share earnings to increase by $0.16, which in turn caused a $4.00 increase in the stock's market price. Shareholders double their money and get to own a bigger piece of the pie.

Understand that as total net earnings increase over time, the reduction in the number of outstanding shares will cause an even larger increase in the market value of the stock. As an example, let us say that in the year 2003, Coca-Cola's total net earnings have increased at an annual rate of 15% over the preceding decade—from $2,176,000,000 in 1993 to $8,403,000,000 in 2003. Now let's run the per share figures for Coca-Cola in 2003 as if it still had the same number of shares it had outstanding in 1984 (3,174,000,000.) We will also run the per share figures for Coca-Cola in 2003, with only 2,604,000,000 shares outstanding, reflecting the share repurchases that took place between 1984 and 1993.

**In 2003 without Share Repurchases:** Total net earnings of $8,403,000,000 ÷ 3,174,000,000 shares = per share earnings of **$2.65 in 2003.** If you multiply $2.65 by a P/E of 25 you get a **per share market price of $66.25** ($2.65 × 25 = $66.25).

**In 2003 with Share Repurchases:** Total net earnings of $8,403,000,000 ÷ 2,604,000,000 shares = per share earnings of **$3.23 in 2003.** If you multiply $3.23 by a P/E of 25 you get a **per share market price of $80.75** ($3.23 × 25 = $80.75).

The difference between the two is **$14.50** ($80.75 - $66.25 = $14.50).

Without the share repurchases, per share earnings will be approximately $2.65, which equates to a market price of $66.25 a share. But with share repurchases the per share earnings in 2003 will be approximately $3.23, which equates to a market price of $80.75 a share. This means that the $1.87 a share in shareholders' equity that was spent retiring Coca-Cola stock between 1984 and 1993, in this hypothetical case, is projected to produce in 2003 an increase of $14.50 in the market price for the stock. This would give the shareholders an approximate annual compounding rate of return of approximately 15% on the $1.87 of their money that Coca-Cola spent buying back its shares.

If Coca-Cola paid out as a dividend the $5.8 billion that it spent on buying back its own stock, the stockholders would have had to pay personal income tax, reducing their take to approximately $4 billion, or $1.26 a share.

So the choice that you the investor have to make is, do you want the $1.26 a share in your pocket or do you want Coca-Cola to spend it on increasing the size of your portion of the Coca-Cola pie?

### Coca-Cola Stock Repurchase Program's Effect on Berkshire's Ownership Interest

Berkshire acquired approximately a 7.8% ownership interest in Coca-Cola in the period from 1987 through 1994. From 1994 to 1999, Coke decreased the number of its outstanding shares from 2.551 billion to 2.460 billion. This caused Berkshire's ownership interest in Coke to increase by approximately

0.33%, from approximately 7.8% in 1994, to approximately 8.13% in 1999 (8.13% - 7.8% = 0.33%). Coke's market capitalization in 1999 was approximately $135.3 billion, which means that Coke's stock repurchases added approximately $444.49 million to Berkshire's net worth without Berkshire's having to invest another dime in Coke ($135.3 billion × 0.0033 = $446.49 million). During this period the stock market increased its valuation of Coke from a price to earnings ratio of 22 in 1994, to a price to earnings ratio of 50 in 1999. For Berkshire and for Warren, Coca-Cola's stock repurchase program turned a good thing into a great thing.

---

## KEY POINTS FROM THIS CHAPTER

- **Through the use of share repurchases it is possible for a company to cause an increase in per share earnings while increasing the ownership interests of the remaining shareholders.**

- **Share repurchases leave the pie the same size while increasing the size of the slice.**

- **Share repurchases make economic sense even at really high share prices.**

---

## Study Questions

Why would a company engage in share repurchases?

Why do shareholders want a company to engage in share repurchases?

How do share repurchase programs make Warren richer?

## Story Problem

If Company A has net earnings of $150 million in 2000, and 800 million shares outstanding, how much does it earn per share? How much will it earn per share if it only has 300 million shares outstanding?

Answer: With 800 million shares outstanding the company will earn $0.18 a share.
With 300 shares outstanding the company will earn $0.50 a share.

# 19: FINANCIAL CALCULATION #10: HOW TO DETERMINE IF PER SHARE EARNINGS ARE INCREASING BECAUSE OF SHARE REPURCHASES

We have discussed how to project the annual compounding growth rate for per share earnings out over a number of years. We have also discussed how a company can increase the annual compounding growth rate on per share earnings through stock repurchase programs. But when you analyze a security, you need to know what is causing any increase in per share earnings. Is it the economic engines of the business that are creating the increase? Or is it financial mechanics? Or is it some combination of both?

You can determine which by comparing the company's actual net earnings annual compounding growth rate against the annual compounding growth rate for per share earnings. Remember that the per share figure is derived from taking the company's net earnings and dividing them by the number of shares the company has outstanding.

In 1999, Gillette had total net earnings of $1,265 million. Divide this by the number of shares outstanding—1,095 million—and you get a per share figure of $1.15. If you decrease the number of shares outstanding to 800 million, you get a per share earnings figure of $1.58. If you increased the number of shares to 1,500 million, per share earnings would drop to $0.84. There is a simple inverse relationship here: Decrease the number of shares and the per share earnings figure goes up. Increase the number of shares and the per share figure goes down.

We've already discussed how management can effectively use capital to increase the shareholders' wealth. Unfortunately management can also hide mediocre results with the same tool.

Let's say in 1990 Company X had net earnings of $100 million and 10 million shares outstanding, which equates to per share earnings of $10 ($100 million ÷ 10 million = $10). Now let's say that by 2000, Company X experienced a decrease in sales and only reports $75 million in net income. Let's also say that over the last ten years Company X has implemented a share repurchase program that has reduced the number of shares that it has outstanding to 5 million shares. This means that in 2000 Company X will report earnings of $15 per share ($75 million ÷ $5 million = $15).

So even though Company X actually had a decline in net earnings from $100 million a year to $75 million, over the ten-year period between 1990 and 2000, the company still reported an increase in per share earnings from $10 to $15 a share.

This means that Company X had an annual growth rate for per share earnings of 4.13%. But actual net earnings had an annual loss of 2.83%. Managers, being the creative devils that they are, use this technique to keep their shareholders in line. Hey, per share earnings increased 4.13% last year! Not bad! Now go back to watching TV and leave us alone.

Sometimes the capital needs of a company are so extreme that instead of buying back its shares it issues more. And more outstanding shares means a decrease in per share earnings. Figure it this way: if you have net earnings of $10 million and 100 million shares outstanding, you have per share earnings of $0.10 a share (10,000,000 ÷ 100,000,000 = 0.10). If you increase the number of shares outstanding to 125 million, you see a decrease in per share earnings to $0.08 a share (10,000,000 ÷ 125,000,000 = 0.08). Just as a decrease in the number of shares outstanding doesn't affect the growth rate for actual net earnings, an increase in the number of shares has no effect either. What changes are per share earnings.

## Summary

Share repurchases can cause an increase in per share earnings even if net earnings don't increase. They can also cause an increase in per share earnings even if there is a decrease in net earnings. One needs to ascertain the annual compounding growth rate for net earnings and then compare it to the annual compounding growth rate for per share earnings, to determine whether it is actual net earnings that are causing the growth in per share earnings or share repurchases are causing the increase or a combination of both.

Shrewd use of share repurchase programs can greatly enhance shareholder wealth but they are no substitute for the rectifying power of actual net earnings growth. When a company suffers a business setback it is the strength of its economic engine, the consumer monopoly, that ultimately determines whether or not the enterprise will rebound and continue to grow, not financial mechanics.

---

# KEY POINTS
# FROM THIS CHAPTER

- **Through the use of share repurchases it is possible for a company to cause an increase in per share earnings while actual net earnings remain the same.**

- **With share repurchases it is also possible for a company to enhance the economic performance of the company.**

- **Share repurchases can sometimes mask poor performance.**

- **Share repurchases can increase your ownership interest in a business without increasing your investment.**

---

## Study Questions

Why would a company that is experiencing a real drop in net income use share repurchases to increase its per share earnings?

Why would a company issue more shares instead of buying them back?

How are share repurchases used to increase shareholders' wealth?

## Story Problem

If Company A in 1990 has 100 million shares outstanding and net earnings of $10 million, how much has it earned per share? If Company A in 2000 has 50 million shares outstanding and net earnings of $8 million, how much has it earned per share? Are Company A's actual net earnings growing or shrinking? Are Company A's per share earnings growing or shrinking?

Answer: In 1990 Company A earned $0.10 a share. In 2000 it earned $0.16 a share. From 1990 to 2000 Company A's actual net earnings shrank, while its per share earnings grew.

## 20: FINANCIAL CALCULATION #11: HOW TO MEASURE MANAGEMENT'S ABILITY TO UTILIZE RETAINED EARNINGS

When a company earns a profit it has to decide what to do with it. As a rule a portion of the profit must be used to replenish capital equipment of the core business that produced the profit. Warren considers these earnings "restricted."

Say Company A earns $1 million in 1992, but anticipates that the following year it will have to replace a generator at its main plant that will cost $400,000. This means that in 1993 the company has to come up with $400,000 to replace the generator, or it is out of business. If the company hasn't saved $400,000, it will have to find a way to raise the money. But Company A earned $1 million in 1992 so at the end of that year, when it is trying to figure out what to do with this $1 million, the company's management will allocate $400,000 of the $1 million in earnings to the purchase of the new generator.

This means that $400,000 of Company A's $1 million in earnings is now restricted. Thus, of the $1 million, management must still decide what to with with the remaining $600,000—either pay it out as a dividend to Company A's shareholders or spend it on new business ventures.

It is the $600,000 in unrestricted earnings that Warren finds interesting. What Company A's management does with it will determine whether Company A grows in value for the shareholders or not.

Warren believes that management should use the unrestricted earnings to give the shareholders the best value. He also believes that management should only retain unrestricted earnings if it can earn a higher rate of return on the unrestricted earnings than the shareholders could earn on the outside.

Let's assume that Company A's management is able to employ the $600,000 in unrestricted earnings in a manner that would earn the company an annual return of 15%. If shareholders received the $600,000 as a dividend, they may not be able to invest it as well. In which case Company A should keep the unrestricted earnings rather than pay them out as a dividend. (Please note: This example forgoes the effects of taxation to keep things simple). Warren believes that a company should retain unrestricted earnings only if it is reasonable to project that the management would do a better job than shareholders would do reinvesting those unrestricted earnings.

If the reverse were true and the shareholders could earn a return of 15% and Company A's management could only reinvest the earnings at a rate of 5%, then it would make more sense to pay out the unrestricted earnings as a dividend to the shareholders.

Our problem as investors is that it is hard to determine whether the management of a company is doing a superior job of allocating its unrestricted earnings. This is because a company with exceptional economics in its core business can produce tons of excess cash and in the process cover up any mistakes that management makes allocating capital. A tremendous business can be so strong that it can hide even inept management.

Inflation also helps hide management's performance by increasing the level of earnings on the core business even though unit sales remain the same. A 10% increase in the price level could equate to a 10% increase in the price of the company's products and a 10% increase in net earnings. If the core business is one that requires very little new capital investment, then this increase in earnings created by inflation could be incorrectly attributed to management's ability to allocate unrestricted earnings.

So that is the problem. How do we as investors measure a company and its management's ability to profitably allocate unrestricted earnings?

There is a simple mathematical way of measuring management's performance. It takes into account retained earnings management has accumulated over a set period of time and then measures management's ability to allocate those retained earnings to more profitable operations.

The formula is simple: We take the *per share amount of earnings retained by a business for a certain period of time, then compare it to any increase in per share earnings that occurred during this same period.*

Let's look at several examples.

In 1989 Gillete made $0.34 a share. This means that all the capital invested in Gillette until the end of 1989 produced $0.34 a share for its owners in 1989. From the end of 1989 through the end of 1999 Gillette had total earnings of $8.67 per share. Of that $8.67, Gillette paid out a total of $3.11 a share in dividends. This means that for that ten-year period Gillette retained earnings of $5.56 a share ($8.67 − $3.11 = $5.56).

So between the end of 1989 and the end of 1999, Gillette earned a total of $8.67 a share, paid out in dividends a total of $3.11 a share, and retained to its capital base a total of $5.56 a share.

Between 1989 and 1999, Gillette's per share earnings rose from $.34 a share to $1.15 a share. We can attribute the 1989 earnings of $0.34 a share to all the capital invested in Gillette up to the end of 1989. We can also argue that the increase in earnings from $0.34 a share in 1989 to $1.15 a share in 1999 was due to Gillette management's excellent job of utilizing the $5.56 a share in earnings that Gillette retained between 1989 and 1999.

If we subtract the 1989 per share earnings of $0.34 from the 1999 per share earnings of $1.15, we find that the difference is $0.81 a share. Thus we can argue that the $5.56 a share that was retained between 1989 and 1999 produced $0.81 in additional per share income for 1999. We could say that the $5.56 in retained earnings earned $0.81 in 1999 for a total return of 14.5% ($0.81 ÷ $5.56 = 14.5%).

Thus we can argue that Gillette's management earned a 14.5% return in 1999 on the $5.56 a share in shareholders' capital that Gillette retained from 1989 to 1999.

Let's compare Gillette to General Motors, a commodity type of business, which had total retained per share earnings of $42.96 between 1989 and 1999, of which $10.30 was paid out in dividends and $32.66 was retained by the company. Per share earnings for General Motors increased from $6.33 in 1989 to $8.50 in 1999. General Motors' management kept $32.66 per share of shareholders' earnings and allocated it in such a manner that per share earnings increased by $2.17. Thus we can argue that the $32.66 a share that was retained between 1989 through 1999 produced $2.17 in additional income for 1999. Let me repeat that. General Motors retained $32.66 of its shareholders' money and only managed to increase per share earnings by $2.17 a share. This equates to a rate of return on retained capital of 6.6% ($2.17 ÷ $32.66 = 6.6%).

Even if we have no idea what business these two companies are in, we can tell that Gillette does a better job of allocating retained capital than General Motors does. In fact, if you had invested $100,000 in General Motors' stock in 1989 and sold it at its high in 1999, you would have had a net profit of $141,025, which equates to an annual compounding rate of return of approximately 9.1%. If you had invested $100,000 in Gillette's stock in 1989 and sold out at its high in 1999, you would have had a net profit of $1,500,000, which equates to an annual compounding rate of approximately 31%. So which stock would you rather own? General Motors, the commodity business, with its annual compounding rate of return of 9.1%, or Gillette, the consumer monopoly, with its annual compounding rate of return of 31%? It's that simple.

This test is not perfect. One must be careful that the per share earnings figures used are not aberrations, but are indicative of all real increases or decreases in the company's earning power. The advantage to this test is that it gives you, the investor, a really fast method of determining whether or not a company and its management have the ability to allocate retained earnings in a fashion that increases the wealth of the company's shareholders.

---

## KEY POINTS
## FROM THIS CHAPTER

- **Consumer monopolies tend to do a better job of allocating retained earnings than commodity type companies do.**

- **The company that does a good job of allocating retained earnings over the long term will make its shareholders a lot more money than those that don't.**

- **Commodity type businesses are able to retain earnings, but because of the high costs of their businesses they are unable to utilize them in a manner that will cause a significant increase in future earnings, which means that their stock price stagnates.**

- **Consumer monopolies are able to retain earnings and utilize them in a manner that results in an increase in net earnings, thus increasing their stock prices and making their stockholders richer.**

---

## Study Questions

Why would you expect retained earnings to add value to a business?

Why, in most cases, do retained earnings fail to add value to a business?

Why are some companies able to allocate retained earnings more profitably than other companies?

## Story Problem

X Corporation, which makes X Bar Candy, from 1990 to the end of 2000 produced total per share earnings of $20, of which $8 was paid out as dividends. This means that between 1990 and 2000 the X Corporation retained $___ a share in shareholder earnings. From 1990 to 2000, per share earnings increased from $1 a share in 1990 to $4 a share in 2000. How much did per share earnings increase? $___. We can argue that X Corporation retained $___ a share in shareholder earnings, which in 2000 produced $___ a share in new earnings, for a rate of return of ___%.

Answers: X Corp. retained $12 a share. From 1990 to 2000 earnings incrseased by $3 a share. This equates to a rate of return of 25% ($3 ÷ $12 = 0.25).

# 21: FINANCIAL CALCULATION #12: THE INTERNET AND WARREN'S SHORT-TERM ARBITRAGE COMMITMENTS

Five years ago, writing a chapter on stock arbitrage would only have been useful to institutional investors like Warren, who could wrangle institutional rates out of the brokerage firms. But with the advent of Internet on-line trading, the days of individual investors paying exorbitant transaction fees are over. The rates on-line trading companies offer are often less than one cent a share. In fact, several on-line trading companies, including American Express, offer free trading with a minimum balance of $100,000. That's right, free trades. In the old days not even the big boys got them for free.

For the arbitrage player this means that the spread between the price that is offered to purchase the company and the price the market is currently offering to sell you the stock can be as narrow as one cent and you would still make money! This is a first in the history of Wall Street. Let's take a look and see how Warren was made big money playing the arbitrage game, which until now was off-limits to the little guys.

## WARREN AND ARBITRAGE

One of Warren's hidden talents is his success in the field of arbitrage, or, as he calls it, "workouts." These arbitrage or workout opportunities arise from corporate sellouts, reorganizations, mergers, spin-offs, and hostile takeovers. Warren prefers to commit capital to investment for the long term, but when no opportunity for long-term investment presents itself, he has found that arbitrage or workout opportunities offer him a vastly more profitable venue for utilizing cash assets than other short-term investments. In fact, over the

153

thirty-some years during which Warren has been actively investing in these types of arbitrage situations, he estimates that his average annual pretax rate of return has been in the neighborhood of 25%. That's real money in anybody's book.

In the early days of the Buffett Partnership, up to 40% of the total partnership funds in any given year were invested in arbitrage or workout situations. In dark years like 1962, when the entire market was headed south, the profits from workouts saved the day. They allowed the partnership to be up + 13.9%, compared to the Dow, which was down −7.6%. (The Buffett Partnership's investments in normal operations actually lost money in 1962. It was the arbitrage/workout profits that turned a disaster into the stuff that financial legends are made of.)

Although there are many types of arbitrage/workouts, or "special situations," as Graham called them, Warren has come to be very comfortable with what Graham called "cash payments on sale or liquidation." In this type of arbitrage, a company sells out its business operations to another entity or decides to liquidate its operations and distribute the proceeds to its security holders.

Warren's purchase in 1988 of 3,342,000 shares of RJR Nabisco stock for $281.8 million after the announcement of the buyout firm KKR's $22 billion bid for the company is a good example of a company selling out to another entity.

Warren's purchase of General Dynamics stock was motivated by the company's announcement that it was going to liquidate certain business properties and disburse the proceeds to its shareholders.

An investment opportunity arises for the arbitrageur when a price spread develops between the announced sale or liquidation price and the market price for the company's stock before the sale or the liquidation.

Say, Company X announces that it has contracted to sell all its stock to Company Y for $110 a share at some future date. But the arbitrageur, because of market volatility, is able to buy the stock for $100 a share before the close of the transaction, so the arbitrageur will make a profit of $10 a share—the difference between the market price paid, $100, and the contracted sale price of $110 ($110 − $100 = $10). The question becomes: When will the transaction close so that the arbitrageur can cash out at $110 a share and make the $10 a share profit?

Thus, the big question is one of time. The more time that elapses between the date that the purchase was announced and the date the transaction actually closes, the smaller your annual rate of return. Let us show you.

If you paid $100 a share and the company was going to sell out in twelve months at $110 a share, your profit would be $10 and your pretax annual rate of return would be 10%. But what would happen if, because of some complication, the transaction didn't close for, say, two years? Your pretax *annual* rate of return would drop to 4.9%.

Likewise, if you got lucky and the transaction closed in six months instead of twelve, then your pretax annual compounding rate of return would jump to 21%.

The arbitrage/workout situation is essentially an investment with a timetable. The amount that you are going to earn is fixed—in our example, $20. The length of time that the security is held determines the pretax annual rate of return. The less time you hold it, the larger the pretax annual rate of return. The longer you hold it, the smaller the rate of return.

There are certain risks to investing in these types of situations. One, as we already discussed, is that the transaction may take much longer than anyone expects. Or the transaction may not occur at all. That is, as we used to say, a major bummer.

There are hundreds of reasons why these transactions may take longer than expected or not at all. Sometimes the shareholders reject the offer; other times the government antitrust people are the party poopers; and sometimes IRS takes an eternity to issue a tax ruling. Anything and everything can go wrong.

Warren protects himself from some of the risk by investing only in situations that have been announced. That sounds like the normal, intelligent thing to do. What kind of fool would invest in a transaction that hasn't been announced? Care to take a guess? You got it. Wall Street! Yes, the Wall Street wizards have worked their brains overtime and figured out that they can make a lot of money by investing in companies that are RUMORED to be takeover candidates. Trading on rumors can mean big profits, but it also means greater risk.

After being involved in literally hundreds of arbitrage workout situations, Warren knows one thing for sure, that an almost certain annual rate of return of 25% is always a better bet than a 100% annual rate of return that may never happen. The gnomes of Wall Street can trade on rumors, but Warren will only invest after the sale or merger has been announced.

During the Buffett Partnership years, from 1957 to 1969, Warren was of the opinion that the arbitrage workout category of investment would produce, year to year, the most steady and absolute profits for the partnership. In years of market decline he learned it gave the partnership a big competitive edge.

You should understand that when the stock market is going down, shareholders and management start to worry about the sinking price of the company's stock, and therefore are more willing to entertain selling out, liquidation, or other forms of reorganization. Thus, when the market starts to sink, the opportunities in the field of arbitrage naturally abound.

## THE GRAHAMIAN EQUATION

Warren learned the arbitrage/workout game from Graham. Graham, who was influenced by Meyer H. Weinstein's classic 1931 treatise on the subject, *Arbitrage in Securities* (Harper Brothers), expounded brilliantly on the subject in his 1951 edition of *Security Analysis*.

Graham noted that in the case of a sale for cash of a going concern, large profits were to be found if the security was bought *before* the announcement. Graham also noted that after the announcement—but before the consummation of the sale—an interesting spread often developed between the market price of the security and the announced sale price. This particular arbitrage is what Warren finds most profitable.

Because of the complexity of the investment and the different variables that come into play, Graham developed a general formula to determine the profit potential of a particular transaction. It is this formula that he taught Warren:

Let:  G = the expected gain in the event of success;
      L = the expected loss in the event of failure;
      C = the expected chances of success, expressed as a percentage;
      Y = the expected time of holding, in years;
      P = the current price of the security.

$$\text{Applied Annual return} = \frac{CG - L(100\% - C)}{YP}$$

The formula takes into account the possibility for loss, which should be weighed into any transaction of this type. Let's take a look at how it works.

### Example of the Use of the Graham Arbitrage Formula

On February 13, 1982, Bayuk Cigars Inc. announced that it had approval from the Justice Department to sell its cigar operations to American Maize Products Co. for $14.5 million, or approximately $7.87 a share. It also announced that it was adopting a plan of liquidation and would distribute the proceeds from the sale to its shareholders.

Shortly after the announcement, Warren bought 5.71% of Bayuk Cigar's outstanding stock for $572,907, or $5.44 a share. Warren was exploiting the spread that had developed between the current market price of $5.44 a share (P) and the future distribution to the shareholders of the proceeds from the sale of Bayuk's assets, which was estimated to be $7.87 a share.

In applying the above Graham equation for arbitrage situations, the first thing Warren did was to calculate his prospective per share profit. He did this by subtracting the sale price of $7.87 a share, minus $5.44, the market price that he paid per share. This equates to a profit potential (G) of $2.43 a share ($7.87 − $5.44 = $2.43).

He then multiplied his potential profit, $2.43, by the chances of success, expressed as a percentage. In this case the deal has been announced and approved by the Justice Department. There is little that can get in the way of its happening. Warren assigned a 90% or better figure for the chances that the transaction would actually be completed (C). Warren then multiplied his profit potential, $2.43, by 90%, which gives him a risk-adjusted profit of $2.18.

Warren then figured out the amount that he would lose if the transaction doesn't take place. If the sale were canceled, the per share price of the stock would probably fall back to the price it was before the sale was announced. If the sale didn't happen, the per share price of Bayuk Cigar's stock would return to $4.50 a share, the price it was before the sale and liquidation were announced. Since Warren paid $5.44 a share, if Bayuk's stock then dropped to $4.50 a share, he would lose $.94 a share (L).

Warren calculated the chances of loss by subtracting the chances of success, 90%, from 100%, which gave him a 10% chance of the transaction not happening. He then multiplied the amount of his projected loss, $.94, by 10%, which gave him a projected loss of $.09.

Warren also estimated the length of time that it would take for the transaction to take place (Y). In liquidating the company's assets, management would have to distribute the proceeds within the company's fiscal year or it would have to pay a capital gains tax. Knowing this, Warren figured the sale would be completed within the year.

The Graham Arbitrage Formula applied to the Bayuk Cigar situation:

(G) = $2.43, the expected gain in
      the event of success;

(L) = $.94, the expected loss in the event of failure;

(C) = 90%, the expected chances
      of success, expressed as a percentage;

(Y) = One year, the expected time
      of holding;

(P) = $5.44, the current price of the security.

Applied         CG − L(100% − C)

$$\text{Annual return} = \frac{\rule{3cm}{0.4pt}}{Y \ P}$$

or

$$\overset{\displaystyle C \quad G \quad L \quad C}{\text{Applied} \qquad 90\% \times \$2.43 - \$.94(100\% - 90\%)}$$

$$\text{Annual return} = \frac{\rule{2.5cm}{0.4pt}}{\underset{1 \times \$5.44}{Y \ P}} = 38\%$$

Warren figured that his annual rate of return would be 38% if the transaction and the liquidation of Bayuk Cigar occurred on schedule. Not too shabby for a short-term commitment of capital.

Warren has played many different arbitrage opportunities. In addition to the Bayuk Cigar and RJR deals, he has owned for arbitrage purposes Texas National Petroleum, Allegis, Lear Siegler Services, Chesebrough-Ponds, Kraft Foods, Interco, Federated, Southland, and Marine Midland Bank, to name just a few. In a given year he may have up to twenty arbitrage positions. Or he may have none.

From a historical perspective Warren discovered that, in the field of arbitrage, the problem of realization of value is alleviated by a firmly established transaction date, which causes the investment to reach its full value at a fixed date. The investor merely has to calculate whether or not the situation affords a sufficient rate of return to merit a commitment of his capital.

## Getting Started

Getting started is as easy as visiting the Web site mergerstat.com, which lists all the major mergers on a daily basis. Write down the company names and stock symbols and keep track of them. If an interesting spread develops, call the company for details about whether the merger is still on and for when. If it is, then run the Graham arbitrage equation to determine whether the rate of return looks good. If it does, move on it. It's an easy game and one that has worked very well for Warren over the years. We think it's one moneymaking technique that every Internet-savvy investor can master.

## A WORD OF WARNING!

A ton of money can be made from stock arbitrage and it is an area of investing that you should seriously consider. But, always remember, as we said earlier, Warren only takes arbitrage positions AFTER THE BUYOUT OR LIQUIDATION HAS BEEN ANNOUNCED. If you do it before the announcement (based on rumor), then you are engaging in the potentially lucrative, but highly dangerous, game of speculative stock arbitrage, a pursuit that has sunk many a big-time player.

## KEY POINTS FROM THIS CHAPTER

- **With arbitrage, Warren was able to produce positive results for his investment partnership even in down years.**
- **Warren will only take arbitrage positions in deals that have been publicly announced.**
- **The Internet trading companies have brought down commission prices to the point that arbitrage is even profitable for individual investors working with small sums of money.**
- **Mergerstat.com lists daily merger activity and is an excellent source of information about publicly announced mergers.**

## Study Questions

Why does Warren only invest in arbitrage situations that have been publicly announced?

How is an arbitrage situation different from a liquidation situation?

## Story Problem

On June 1, 2001, Y Corp. announces that it will buy Z Corp. for $25 a share and the transaction will be completed on December 31, 2002. If you determine that there is a 100% chance that this transaction will close on schedule and you buy Z Corp's stock on June 1, 2001, for $20 a share and tender it on December 31, 2001, to Y Corp. for $25 a share, what is your rate of return on this transaction? What would be your relative annual rate of return?

Answer: Your rate of return on the investment is 25%.
Your relative rate of return from an annual perspective is 50%.

# 22: DOING IT YOURSELF BUFFETTOLOGY WORKSHEET

You've done your homework and now it is time to take the car out for a test drive. It's time for you to do it yourself. We have designed the following list of questions to help you get your mental juices flowing and to give you a format to work with as you work through the thought process that Warren uses.

1. **Does the company have an identifiable consumer monopoly?** Yes or no? If yes, describe it in as simple manner as you can, as you would to a seven-year-old child. Warren likes to keep things simple. If you can't explain it to a child, then the consumer monopoly probably doesn't exist. If you can't find a consumer monopoly, keep your powder dry until you do. Waiting for the perfect pitch never bothered Warren.

Describe the consumer monopoly you're eyeing:

_____

_____

_____

_____

2. **Do you understand how it works?** Warren believes that if you don't understand how the product works you will never be able to determine the chances of its becoming obsolete. Product obsolescence is a real and legitimate fear that Warren respects. Warren keeps that fear at bay by fully understanding the nature of the business in which he is investing. If you can't explain a business that you are interested in, move on. Find something that you do understand.

Explain how the product works:

_____

_____

_____

_____

**3. If the company in question does have a consumer monopoly, the next question is: What is the chance that it will become obsolete or replaced in the next twenty years?** Warren likes to ask himself this question: Will people more than likely be using this product in twenty years? If the answer is yes, continue on with the analysis. If not, stop, go to a movie, and start again in the morning.

Explain why this product won't be obsolete in twenty years:

_____

_____

_____

_____

**4. Is the company a conglomerate?** If it is, you need to know whether it has acquired other consumer monopolies or has diversified into a group of weaker commodity type businesses. Remember, the cyclical nature of the commodity type business might just offer you an opportunity to buy the company on the cheap because the market is undervaluing the long-term value of the consumer monopoly. If it looks like a great business or a great collection of good businesses, go fetch yourself a glass of your favorite drink and settle in for some serious analysis.

If the company is a conglomerate, list which businesses are consumer monopolies and which are commodity types. Figure out which direction management is headed. Is it consumer monopoly minded and allocating capital to buy more consumer monopolies, or is it fixated on the commodity side of the business and headed in that direction?

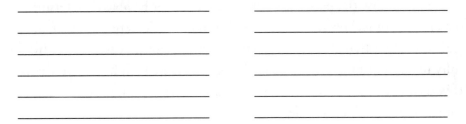

| Comsumer Monopolies | Commodity Type Businesses |
| --- | --- |
| _____ | _____ |
| _____ | _____ |
| _____ | _____ |
| _____ | _____ |
| _____ | _____ |

**5. What is the company's earnings per share history?** Is it consistently strong or consistently weak? If it is strong, continue the analysis. If it's weak, you need to ask yourself whether this is a onetime event or something that will become the norm. If it is a onetime event, continue. (Remember that onetime solvable problems may offer a chance to make a fantastic profit). If weak or erratic earnings are a routine occurrence, then stop your analysis and save your cash until Mr. Market serves up something better to swing at.

If earnings appear to be consistently strong, you should gather the company's EPS figures for the last ten years from *Value Line* or one of the on-line sources already mentioned and calculate its annual compounding growth rate for that period using the calculation below.

| Actual Year | | | Per Share Earnings |
|---|---|---|---|
| 1. 1990 | | ____ → | **Present value (base year)** |
| 2. 1991 | one | ____ | Financial calculation for use with TI BA-35 |
| 3. ____ | two | ____ | Solar Calculator: **Earnings per share growth rate.** |
| 4. ____ | three | ____ | Use the base year's per share earnings as the |
| 5. ____ | four | ____ | present value (PV); year ten as your future value |
| 6. ____ | five | ____ | (FV); and 10 as your number of years. Hit the |
| 7. ____ | six | ____ | compute key (CPT) and then the interest key |
| 8. ____ | seven | ____ | (%i) and your annual compounding growth rate |
| 9. ____ | eight | ____ | for per share will be calculated. |
| 10. ____ | nine | ____ | |
| 11. ____ | ten | ____ → | **Future value** |

↑

**Number of years from present value base year**

**6. Is the company consistently earning a high return on shareholders' equity?** A company that doesn't earn high returns on shareholders' equity will not grow over the long term at a sufficient rate to make you rich. You need a fast and powerful ship to carry you across the water. This means that you need a return on shareholders' equity of 15% or better. If the company doesn't get high returns on shareholders' equity you should put down your pen and take a walk. If it does, get out your *Value Line* and gather together the return on shareholders' equity figures for the last ten years and calculate the average.

| | <u>Year</u> | <u>Return on Shareholders' Equity</u> |
|---|---|---|
| 1. | ____ | ____ |
| 2. | ____ | ____ |
| 3. | ____ | ____ |
| 4. | ____ | ____ |
| 5. | ____ | ____ |
| 6. | ____ | ____ |
| 7. | ____ | ____ |
| 8. | ____ | ____ |
| 9. | ____ | ____ |
| 10. | ____ | ____ |

Financial Calculation for use with TI BA-35 Solar Calculator: **Average Return on Shareholders' Equity.** Add up the return on equity figures over the last ten years and then divide by 10.

Average Return on Shareholders' Equity = _____

**7. Is the company conservatively financed?** In order for a company to have the economic power to pull it out of any business difficulties it may encounter, it needs to have plenty of financial power. Consumer monopolies usually create such great wealth for their owners that they are long-term debt free or close to it. Standard debt to shareholders' equity ratios give a poor picture of the business's financial strength, in that shareholders' equity is seldom used to extinguish debt. The earning power of a business is the only real judge of a company's ability to service and retire its debt. You need to ask yourself this question: How many years of past net earnings would be required to pay off all the long-term debt of the business in the current year?

Total long-term debt in the current year _____ divided by total net earnings in the current year _____ equals _____ years' earnings needed to pay off long-term debt.

**8. Is the company in question actively buying back its own shares?** The repurchasing of shares is one of Warren's favorite tricks to increase his ownership in a company without having to invest any more of his own money. (*Value Line* is one of the few investment services that provide this information.)

Take the number of shares outstanding ten years ago _____ and subtract from it the number of shares outstanding in the current year _____, which will give the shares the company has purchased over the last ten years _____. A negative number indicates the number of shares that the company has added to its outstanding shares. Warren is looking for a decrease in the number of shares outstanding.

**9. Is the company free to raise prices with inflation?** An interesting question that requires you do a little investigative work. If the item that the company is selling cost the same as it did twenty years ago, you are more than likely dealing with a commodity type business and should pass. If the price of the product has risen on an average of at least 4% a year, over the last twenty years, then you can bet the farm that it's the kind of business that can raise prices along with inflation.

Financial Calculation for use with TI BA-35 Solar Calculator: **Company's Ability to Raise Prices with Inflation.** Use price of the product twenty years ago as your present value (PV); the current price of the product as your future value (FV); and 20 as your number of years. Hit the compute key (CPT) and then the interest key (%i) and your annual compounding growth rate in price for the product will be calculated. (Note: If you get a negative number it means that you are probably looking at a commodity type business and should move on.)

**Annual growth rate of product's price _____.**

## PRICE ANALYSIS

**10. Is the company's stock price suffering from a market panic, a business recession, or an individual calamity that is curable?** As we discussed, these types of situations usually offer the best prices. If you can't buy during one of these events, then there is a good chance that you are paying full price for the stock. If you want to get rich you have to learn how to exploit a bad news situation and the stock market's short-sightedness.

**11. What is the initial rate of the investment and its expected annual rate of growth? How does it compare to rate of return being paid on United States treasury bonds?** Take the company's current per share earnings and divide it by the current market price of a single share. This will give you the investment's initial rate of return. Couple that with the per share earnings growth rate (which you have calculated) and you have the **investment's initial rate of return and its expected annual growth rate.** (With Warren's 1988 purchase of Coca-Cola stock he determined he was getting 6.89% initial rate of return, which would increase as Coca-Cola's per share earnings grew at an estimated rate of between 17% to 19%). You then compare the investment's initial rate of return and expected growth rate to the rate of return being paid on United States treasury bonds. If the treasuries look juicer, the stock might be overpriced.

**Initial rate of return: _____   Growth rate: _____**
**Rate of return on U.S. treasury bonds: _____**

**12. The company's stock as an equity/bond calculation:** Take the company's average annual per share return on shareholders' equity value for the last ten years (see page 164) _____ and subtract the average annual percentage that is paid out as a dividend _____. Use the resulting difference as the rate of growth that the company's shareholders' equity will grow at _____.

Use the company's per share shareholders' equity value in the current year _____ as the present value (PV) and then use the calculated rate of growth for shareholders' equity as the rate of interest (%i). Then punch in 10 for the number of years out that you want to make your projection (N) and then hit the CPT key, followed by the future value key (FV). This will calculate the future per share value of the company's shareholders' equity _____.

To determine the future selling price of the company's stock, take the per share value of shareholders' equity _____ and multiply it by the average return on shareholders' equity _____. This will give you the company's projected future per share earnings _____. Then multiply the projected future earning _____ by the company's average annual price to earnings ratio for the last ten years _____. This will give you the company's per share projected future trading price _____.

Using the company's current market price as your present value (PV) _____ and the projected future trading price as the future value (FV) _____ and the number of years between the two _____ for the (N) key. Then hit the CPT key and then the %i key, which calculates the projected annual compounding rate of return that the investment will produce _____.

**Average annual growth rate for shareholders' equity for the last ten years** _____.
**Average percentage paid out as a dividend** _____.
**Company's shareholders' equity per share in the current year** _____.
**Company's average annual price to earnings ratio** _____.
**Projected growth rate of shareholders' equity over the next ten years**

_____.

**Projected future trading price of the company's stock** _____.
**Current trading price for the company's stock** _____.

**13. Projecting an annual compounding rate of return using the historical annual per share earnings growth figure:** To calculate the projected annual compounding rate of return on an investment purchased in 2000 and sold during 2010, first determine the annual compounding per share growth from 1990 to 2000.

**Per Share Earnings in 1990** _____. **Per Share Earnings in 2000** _____. Use the 1990 per share earnings as the present value, 2000 per share earnings as the future value, and 10 for the number of years. Then hit the CPT key and the %i key, which will give you the company's per share annual compounding growth rate for that period _____.

Now use the company's per share earnings 2000 for your present value (PV), the company's per share annual compounding growth rate for the period between 1990 and 2000 as the interest rate (%i), and 10 for the number of years. Hit the CPT key and then the future value (FV) key, which will the projected per share earnings of the company for the year 2010_____.

Take the projected per share earnings of the company for the year 2010 _____and multiply it by the average annual price to earnings ratio for the period between 1990 and 2000. This will give you the projected trading price for the company's stock in 2010 _____.

| <u>Year</u> | | | <u>Stock Price</u> | |
|------|------|------|------|------|
| 12. <u>2000</u> | | ____ | → **Present value base year** Financial calculation for |
| 13. <u>2001</u> | one | ____ | use with TI BA-35 Solar Calculator: **Projecting** |
| 14. <u>2002</u> | two | ____ | **the Annual Compounding Rate of Return that** |
| 15. <u>2003</u> | three | ____ | **the investment will earn.** Take the stock's current |
| 16. <u>2004</u> | four | ____ | trading price and use it as your present value |
| 17. <u>2005</u> | five | ____ | (PV). Use the projected future trading price of |
| 18. <u>2006</u> | six | ____ | the stock as your future value (FV). Ten for your |
| 19. <u>2007</u> | seven | ____ | number of years (N) and then hit the CPT key |
| 20. <u>2008</u> | eight | ____ | and the interest key (%i). This will give you the |
| 21. <u>2009</u> | nine | ____ | projected compounding annual rate of return |
| | | | that the investment will produce. |
| 22. <u>2010</u> | ten | ____ | → **Future Value** |

      ↑

**Number of Years from Present Value Base Year**


## Do You Make the Buy?

To buy or not to buy is always the question. If the company that you are investigating is a consumer monopoly and you can buy it at a price that make business sense, then you should jump on it. If that same consumer monopoly is selling at too high a price, you should wait for a stock market correction, industry recession, or business calamity to create a more attractive situation. If it isn't a consumer monopoly, then you should put the company out of your mind, go for a long walk, and then renew your search.

## 23: BRINGING IT ALL TOGETHER: THE CASE STUDIES

The following case studies use Warren's techniques to value companies in which he has made investments. These case studies, which include Gannett Corp., Freddie Mac, and McDonald's Corp., appeared in the original edition of *Buffettology*. They are of interest here because it is now possible to see whether Warren's original projections as presented in *Buffettology* were accurate. All three of these companies have split their stock since these case studies first appeared in *Buffettology*. For the sake of clarity and cross-comparison of projections with actual present-day results, we've adjusted the historical numbers to reflect these splits.

The format for each case study is the same, with slight variations in the mathematical portion of the price analysis and projection of the expected annual compounding rate of return. We do this in order to give some diversity to the analysis process and to show you some of the different applications and perspectives the financial calculations you read about in the preceding chapters can provide.

### CASE STUDY NUMBER ONE: GANNETT CORPORATION, 1994

Warren's love affair with the newspaper business probably started when he was a boy. He lived in Washington, D.C., and had a *Washington Post* newspaper route. As you've read, he later took a sizable ownership position in that company.

In the summer of 1994, during the middle of an advertising recession, Warren began to buy large blocks of the Gannett Corporation, a newspaper holding company. He eventually spent $335,216,000 for 13,709,000 shares of Gannett's common stock. This equates to a split-adjusted purchase price of $24.45 a share. Let's examine what he found so enticing. (Please note: Gannett Corporation's stock split two for one in 1997. To assist in comparing our earlier projected results in *Buffettology* with present-day actual results, we have adjusted the historical figures to reflect the two-for-one split.)

## Doing Your Detective Work

The scuttlebutt work on this one is easy. We all know *USA Today,* a Gannett newspaper that you can find on any newsstand in America.

A check of *The Value Line Investment Survey* tells us that Gannett publishes 190 newspapers in thirty-eight states and U.S. territories. Its two largest publications are *The Detroit News* (circ. 312,093) and *USA Today* (circ. 2.1 million). Gannett also owns thirteen radio stations and fifteen network-affiliated TV stations.

Once you have assembled the financial information and thoroughly reviewed it, it's time to work through our questions. (All the financial information found in this and the other case studies was retrieved from Warren's favorite source—*Value Line Investment Survey.*)

1. Does the company have any IDENTIFIABLE CONSUMER MONOPOLIES OR BRAND NAME PRODUCTS, or does it sell a commodity type of product? Newspapers, radio and TV stations, we know, are good businesses. A newspaper can be a great business if it is the only game in town—less competition means bigger advertising bucks for the owners. The majority of Gannett Corporation's newspapers are the only game in town! Nice.

2. Do you UNDERSTAND HOW IT WORKS? This is another of those cases about which you, the consumer/investor, have intimate knowledge. You're stuck in an out-of-town airport with nothing to do, so you go to the newsstand and buy a newspaper. Which one do you buy? The local paper? No. They may have great coverage of local political issues, but you don't really care. But, hey, there's *USA Today,* and it has national news!

3. Is the company CONSERVATIVELY FINANCED? A check of the debt to shareholders' equity indicates that in 1994 the company had a total long-term debt of $767 million and a little over $1.8 billion in shareholders' equity. Though not debt free, the company's strong

earnings in 1994 of $465 million show that Gannett could pay off its entire debt burden in just two years.

A glance at the yearly per share earnings figures indicates that—

| Year | Earnings |
|------|----------|
| 1984 | $0.70 |
| 1985 | $0.79 |
| 1986 | $0.86 |
| 1987 | $0.99 |
| 1988 | $1.13 |
| 1989 | $1.24 |
| 1990 | $1.18 |
| 1991 | $1.00 |
| 1992 | $1.20 |
| 1993 | $1.36 |
| 1994 | $1.62 |

—they are strong and show an upward trend. That's what we are looking for.

4. Are the EARNINGS of the company STRONG and do they show an UPWARD TREND? Earnings in 1994 were $1.62 a share and have been growing at an annual compounding rate of 8.75% for the period of 1984 to 1994, and at a rate of 5.4% for the period from 1989 to 1994. Earnings can be considered very stable, increasing every year from 1984 to 1994 with the exception of 1990 and 1991, when the entire publishing and media industry was experiencing a recession due to weakening advertising rates. Remember, a *general* recession in an industry is often a buying opportunity.

5. A review of the company's annual report indicates that the company allocates capital only to those businesses within its REALM OF EXPERTISE, which in this case is the media industry.

6. Further investigation indicates that the company has been buying back its shares. It has bought back 42.4 million of its outstanding shares in the period of 1988 through 1994. This is a sign that management utilizes capital to increase shareholder value when it is possible.

7. The way in which management has spent the retained earnings of the company appears to have increased the per share earnings and therefore, SHAREHOLDER VALUE.

*Value Line* shows us that from 1984 to 1994, Gannett had retained earnings of $5.82 a share. Per share earnings grew by $0.92 a share, from $0.70 a share at the end of 1984 to $1.62 by the end of 1994. Thus, we can argue that the retained earnings of $5.82 a share produced in 1994 an increase in after-tax corporate income of $0.92, which equates to a 15.8% rate of return on the $5.82 a share of retained earnings ($.92 ÷ 5.82 = 15.8%).

8.  A further check of *Value Line* indicates that the company's RETURN ON SHAREHOLDERS' EQUITY IS ABOVE AVERAGE. As we know, Warren considers it a good sign when a business can earn above-average returns on shareholders' equity. An average return on shareholders' equity for American corporations during the last thirty years is approximately 12%. The return on shareholders' equity for Gannett for the last ten years looks like this—

| Year | R.O.E. |
|------|--------|
| 1984 | 19.6% |
| 1985 | 19.9% |
| 1986 | 19.3% |
| 1987 | 19.8% |
| 1988 | 20.4% |
| 1989 | 19.9% |
| 1990 | 18.3% |
| 1991 | 19.6% |
| 1992 | 21.9% |
| 1993 | 20.8% |
| 1994 | 25.5% |

—which gives Gannett an average annual rate of return on shareholders' equity for the last eleven years of 20.4%. But more important than averages is the fact that the company has earned consistently high returns on shareholders' equity, which indicates that management is doing an excellent job in profitably allocating retained earnings to new projects.

9.  IS THE COMPANY FREE TO ADJUST PRICES TO INFLATION? Newspapers used to cost a dime, now they cost 50 cents to a dollar. But newspapers and TV stations make their real money by selling advertising. If you own the only newspaper in town, you can raise advertising rates and there is not much in the way of alternatives for people to switch to. As noted earlier, classified advertising, supermarkets, auto dealers, and entertainment businesses, such as movie theaters,

are reliant upon advertising in the local newspaper. As a whole, we can assume that Gannett adjusts its prices to inflation without running the risk of losing sales.

10.  DO OPERATIONS REQUIRE LARGE CAPITAL EXPENDITURES TO CONSTANTLY UPDATE THE COMPANY'S PLANT AND EQUIPMENT? As we discussed earlier, all the benefits of earning tons of money can be offset by a company constantly having to make large capital expenditures in order to stay competitive. Newspapers and broadcast stations are the foundation of Gannett's success. Printing presses run for years before they wear out and TV and radio stations only need an occasional new transmitter. So once their initial infrastructure is in place, expenditures on capital equipment are kept to a minimum.

This means that when Gannett makes money, it doesn't have to turn around and spend it on research and development or upgrading plant and equipment. Gannett can instead buy more newspapers and radio stations or it can use the excess cash to buy back its own stock, making Gannett's shareholders richer and richer.

## Summary of Data

Since Warren gets positive responses to the above key questions, he concludes that Gannett is a company that he can fit into his "realm of confidence," and that its earnings can be predicted with a fair degree of certainty. But a positive response to these questions DOES NOT mean it's an automatic buy. Once a company is identified as THE TYPE OF BUSINESS we want to be in, we still have to calculate whether the market price for the stock will allow a return equal to or better than our other options.

## Price Analysis

As we have said and will say again, IDENTIFY THE COMPANY with the consumer monopoly and then LET THE MARKET PRICE DETERMINE THE BUY DECISION.

## INITIAL RATE OF RETURN AND RELATIVE VALUE TO GOVERNMENT BONDS

In the case of Gannett, the per share earnings in 1994 were $1.62 a share. Divide $1.62 by the long-term government bond interest rate for 1994, approximately 7%, and you get a relative value of $23.14 a share. This means that if you paid $23.14 for a share of Gannett, you would be getting a return equal to what was being offered on government bonds. In 1994 Gannett stock was trading for anywhere from $23.10 to $29.50 a share. Warren paid an average price of $24.45 a share.

With 1994 earnings coming in at $1.62 a share, if you had paid $24.45 a share, you would be getting an estimated initial rate of return of 6.6%. A review of Gannett's per share earnings growth rate for the last ten years indicates that it has been growing at an annual compounding rate of 8.75%. Thus, you can ask yourself this question: What would I rather own—$24.45 worth of a government bond with a static rate of return of 7% or a Gannett Corporation equity/bond with an initial rate of return of 6.6%, which has a coupon that is projected to grow at a rate of 8.75% a year?

## Gannett Company's Stock as an Equity/Bond

From a return on shareholders' equity standpoint, we can argue that in 1994 Gannett had a per share equity value of $6.52; if Gannett can maintain its average rate of return on shareholders' equity of 20.4% over the next ten years and retain approximately 60% of that return, then per share equity value should grow at an annual rate of approximately 12.24% (60% of 20.4 equals 12.24%), to approximately $20.68 a share in Year 10, 2004. (On your Texas Instruments BA-35 Solar calculator, punch in $6.52 as the present value (PV); 10 for the number of years (N); 12.24 for the annual rate of interest (%i); hit the CPT button and then the future value button (FV), and $20.68 will appear as your future value.)

If per share equity value is $20.68 in Year 10, 2004, and Gannett is still earning a 20.4% return on shareholders' equity, then Gannett should report per share earnings of $4.22 a share ($20.68 × .204 = $4.21). If Gannett is trading at its low P/E for the last ten years, 15, the stock should have a market price of approximately $63.15 a share ($4.21 × 15 = $63.15). Multiplied by the ten-year high P/E of 23, you get a per share market price of $96.83 ($4.21 × 23 = $96.83). Add in the projected total dividend pool of $11.92 a share earned from 1994 to 2004 and you get a projected total pretax annual compounding rate of return on your initial investment of $24.45 a share of somewhere between 11.87% and 16.09% for the ten-year period.

### Projecting an Annual Compounding Rate of Return Using the Historical Annual per Share Earnings Growth Figure

Warren can calculate that if per share earnings continue to grow at a rate of 8.75% annually and if Gannett continues to pay out dividends at a rate of 40% of per share earnings, then the following per share earnings and dividend disbursement picture will develop over the next ten years:

| Year | Earnings | Dividends |
|------|----------|-----------|
| 1995 | $1.76 | $ 0.70 |
| 1996 | $1.91 | $ 0.76 |
| 1997 | $2.08 | $ 0.83 |
| 1998 | $2.26 | $ 0.90 |
| 1999 | $2.46 | $ 0.98 |
| 2000 | $2.67 | $ 1.07 |
| 2001 | $2.91 | $ 1.16 |
| 2002 | $3.16 | $ 1.26 |
| 2003 | $3.44 | $ 1.37 |
| 2004 | $3.74 | $ 1.49 |
|      |          | $10.52 |

This means that in the year 2004 Warren can project that Gannett will have per share earnings of $3.74. If Gannett is trading at the lowest price to earnings ratio that it has had in the last ten years—15—then we can calculate that market price will be $56.10 ($3.74 × 15 = $56.10). Add in the pretax dividend pool of $10.52 and our total pretax return jumps to $66.62 a share ($56.10 + $10.52 = $66.62).

If it is trading at the highest P/E that it has had in the last ten years, 23, then we can calculate that the market price for the stock will be $86.02 in the year 2004. Add in the pretax dividend pool of $10.52 and our total pretax return becomes $96.54 ($86.02 + $10.52 = $96.54).

If you were Warren and you had spent $24.45 a share for your Gannett stock in 1994, using this method, you could project that in ten years it would be worth dividends somewhere between $66.62 and $96.54 a share. This equates to a pretax annual compounding rate of return of somewhere between 10.55% and 14.72%. (You can get these figures by taking out the Texas Instruments BA-35 calculator and punching in $24.45 for the present value (PV), 10 for the number of years (N); and either $66.62 or $96.54 for the future value (FV). Hit the CPT key followed by i%; and, presto, your annual compounding rate of return will appear—either 10.55% or 14.72%).

## Summary of Analysis

In the summer and fall of 1994 Warren bought approximately 13,708,000 shares of Gannett common stock for $24.45 a share, for a total purchase price of $335,216,000. When Warren bought the stock he could argue that he had just bought a Gannett equity/bond with a yield of 6.5% that with a coupon projected to grow at a rate of approximately 8.75% a year. He could also figure that if he held the stock for ten years, his projected pretax annual compounding rate of return would be between 10.55% and 16.09%.

This means that in ten years' time his investment of $335,216,000 in Gannett will be worth in pretax terms somewhere between $913,226,960 and $1,490,745,000.

## How Accurate Were Warren's Gannett Projections?

Just how good are these projections? Well, we have actual figures through 1999 to check against. Let's take a look and see just how well Warren has done.

### PROJECTED EARNINGS COMPARED TO ACTUAL EARNINGS

| Year | Projected Earnings | Actual Earnings | Margin of Error |
|------|--------------------|-----------------|-----------------|
| 1995 | $1.76 | $1.71 | −2.84% |
| 1996 | $1.91 | $1.89 | −1   % |
| 1997 | $2.08 | $2.50 | +20.2% |
| 1998 | $2.26 | $2.86 | +26.5% |
| 1999 | $2.46 | $3.30 | +34.1% |

As you can see, Gannett's actual results (as reported in *Value Line*) have surpassed our projections in three of the last five years, with our margin of error ranging from –2.84% to +34.1%. Per share earnings during this period grew at an annual rate of 15.29% as opposed to our projected 8.75%. The stock market, in 2000, seeing this performance, has bid up Gannett's shares into the $70 a share range. Warren paid $24.45 a share in 1994. If he sold it in 2000 for $70 a share his annual pretax compounding rate of return, excluding dividends, would be approximately 19.1%. This surpasses our best-case projection by about three percentage points! With a consumer monopoly, things often work out better than projected, which has Warren smiling all the way to the bank.

## CASE NUMBER TWO: FEDERAL HOME LOAN MORTGAGE CORPORATION, 1992

Warren's involvement with the banking industry led him to the doorsteps of the Federal Home Loan Mortgage Corporation, popularly known as Freddie Mac. Freddie Mac is in the business of securitizing and guaranteeing mortgages. When you take out a mortgage with your local bank and you sign that little piece of paper obligating you to pay the bank so much a month, the bank, more often than not, will sell that loan to Freddie Mac. Freddie Mac, in turn, will package your mortgage together with a group of other mortgages that it has bought. Freddie Mac then sells interests in that pool of mortgages, which includes your mortgage, to individual investors. When you pay interest on your mortgage, your interest payment ends up in the hands of the investors who bought interests in the pool of mortgages that contains your mortgage. On Wall Street these securitized pools of mortgages are called "mortgage-backed bonds."

In 1988, when Freddie Mac began being traded publicly, Berkshire acquired 4% of the company through a Berkshire subsidiary, Wesco Financial. In 1992, with Freddie Mac trading at or near its all-time high, Warren increased Berkshire's holdings in Freddie Mac by 34,844,400 shares. He paid approximately $337 million or $9.67 a share for this increase in ownership. At the end of 1992 Berkshire owned 9% of Freddie Mac's outstanding shares.

The subject of our second case study will be Berkshire's 1992 increase in its holdings of Freddie Mac stock. The focus of our inquiry is the nature of the business economics of Freddie Mac in 1992 that compelled Warren to add to his position. (Please note that Freddie Mac split its stock four for one in 1997. All historical figures have been adjusted to reflect this split.)

### Doing Your Detective Work

The SCUTTLEBUTT on this one WOULD NOT BE easy. Although it is a visible stock, it is unlikely that you will ever have anything to do with the company in real life.

*Value Line* covers the stock and it is followed by a number of investment houses. A check of the business periodicals and a call to the company for annual reports and 10-Ks will supply you with sufficient information to work through our list of questions.

1. Does the company have any IDENTIFIABLE CONSUMER MONOPOLIES OR BRAND NAME PRODUCTS? Although

mortgages are a commodity type product, Freddie Mac, along with a similar company known as Fannie Mae, are essentially government-sanctioned entities created by Congress to raise money to help prospective homeowners acquire mortgages. In the process, Freddie Mac and Fannie Mae have developed a quasi-monopoly on this segment of the market.

2. Do you UNDERSTAND HOW IT WORKS? Probably not at first glance, but after a little investigation it is a fairly easy business to comprehend. It is not technology driven and the demand for mortgages is enormous and isn't going to evaporate overnight. Remember, one of Warren's rules is that you understand the business that you are investing in. Warren understands Freddie Mac's business, you may not. But there are probably a few businesses that you understand that Warren doesn't. Warren has said that he doesn't understand the drug industry and therefore is uncomfortable investing in it. Yet, if you are a doctor or a druggist, it may be an industry that you fully understand and therefore are very comfortable with. A person who knows a lot about computers can tell you which company has a monopoly and which company is manufacturing a commodity type product. A housewife or house-husband can tell you a great deal about brand name products at the local supermarket. You get the picture. If you don't understand it, find one that you do.

3. Is the company CONSERVATIVELY FINANCED? No. However, Freddie Mac's liabilities are offset by corresponding assets that are highly liquid—mortgages. But, since it does enjoy "government agency status," any financial problems would draw the immediate attention of the United States Congress. And it has a BIG checkbook—namely American taxpayers—to help see its little brother through hard times. Still, if there were considerable defaults on the underlying mortgages in the pools, then it's conceivable that Freddie Mac could find itself in trouble.

4. Are the EARNINGS of the company STRONG—WITH AN UPWARD TREND? A check of the company's earnings indicates that it has been growing at a rate of 17.6% compounded annually from 1986 to 1992, a period of six years. Earnings can be considered very stable, increasing every year for the last six years.

| Year | Earnings |
|------|----------|
| 1986 | $0.31 |
| 1987 | $0.38 |
| 1988 | $0.48 |
| 1989 | $0.55 |
| 1990 | $0.58 |
| 1991 | $0.77 |
| 1992 | $0.82 |

A look at the yearly per share earnings indicates that they are strong and show an upward trend, which is what we are looking for.

5. A review of the company's annual report indicates that the company allocates capital only to those business that are within its REALM OF EXPERTISE. In this case that means the mortgage-backed securities industry.

6. Further investigation indicates that the company has not been buying back its shares. Nor has it been issuing new shares for acquisitions. (Please note: In 1995 Freddie Mac started a stock buyback program).

7. The manner in which management has spent the retained earnings of the company appears to have increased the per share earnings and therefore SHAREHOLDER VALUE.

From the end of 1986 through 1992, Freddie Mac retained earnings of $2.75 a share. Per share earnings grew by $0.51 a share, from $0.31 a share at the end of 1986 to $0.82 by the end of 1992. Thus, we can argue that the retained earnings of $2.75 a share produced in 1992 an after–corporate income tax return of $0.51, which equates to an 18.5% rate of return.

8. The company's RETURN ON SHAREHOLDERS' EQUITY IS ABOVE AVERAGE. As we know, Warren considers it a good sign when a business can earn above average returns on shareholders' equity. An average return on shareholders' equity for American corporations over the last thirty years is approximately 12%. The return on shareholders' equity for Freddie Mac for the period between 1986 and 1992 looks like this—

| Year | R.O.E. |
|------|--------|
| 1986 | 25.9% |
| 1987 | 25.5% |
| 1988 | 24.1% |
| 1989 | 22.8% |
| 1990 | 19.4% |
| 1991 | 21.6% |
| 1992 | 17.4% |

—an average return on shareholders' equity for those seven years of 22.3%. The company earned consistently high returns on shareholders' equity, which indicates that management is doing an excellent job of allocating retained earnings and expanding the business.

9. IS THE COMPANY FREE TO ADJUST PRICES TO INFLATION? Inflation causes housing prices to rise. Increased housing prices mean bigger mortgages. Bigger mortgages means that Freddie Mac gets a larger pie to cut from, which means increased profits. Look at it this way; if you charge 6% to raise $100 million in mortgage money, you make $6 million. If prices double and the $100 million become $200 million and you charge 6%, you make $12 million. The bigger the numbers, the more money Freddie Mac makes.

10. DO THE OPERATIONS REQUIRE LARGE CAPITAL EXPENDITURES TO CONSTANTLY UPDATE THE COMPANY'S PLANT AND EQUIPMENT? As we discussed earlier, all the benefits of earning tons of money can be offset by a company constantly having to make large capital expenditures to keep pace with competitors.

Freddie Mac is in the business of securitizing pooled mortgages, which requires very little in the way of capital equipment or research and development. They can expand operations at will with nominal plant expansion. Large capital expenditures are not needed to update the company's plant and equipment.

## Summary of Data

Since Warren gets positive responses to the above key questions, he concludes that Freddie Mac is a company that he can fit into his "realm of confidence" and that its gearnings can be predicted with a fair degree of certainty. But a positive response to these questions DOES NOT invoke an automatic buy response. Once a company is identified as THE TYPE OF BUSINESS we want to be in, then we still have to calculate the company's intrinsic value and determine whether the market price for the stock will allow a return equal to or better than our other options.

## Price Analysis

Once again, IDENTIFY THE COMPANY and then LET THE MARKET PRICE DETERMINE THE BUY DECISION. We do it this way BECAUSE THE PRICE YOU PAY DETERMINES YOUR RATE OF RETURN.

### Initial Rate of Return and Relative Value to Government Bonds

In 1992 Freddie Mac reported earnings of $0.82 a share. Divide $0.82 by the long-term government bond interest rate for 1992, which was 7.39%, and you get a relative value of $11.09 share. In 1992 you could have bought Freddie Mac stock for between $8.45 and $12.32 a share.

With 1992 earnings of $0.82 a share, if you paid what Warren paid for the stock—an average price of $9.67 a share—you would be getting an estimated initial rate of return of 8.5% ($0.82 ÷ $9.67 = 8.5%).

If you run the equation to determine Freddie Mac's per share earnings growth rate for the last eight years you would find that it has been growing at an annual compounding rate of 17.6%. Thus, you can ask yourself this question: What would I rather own—$11.09 worth of a government bond with a static rate of return of 7.39% or a Freddie Mac equity/bond with an initial rate of return of 8.5%, which has a coupon that is projected to increase at an annual compounding rate of 17.6%?

### Freddie Mac's Stock as an Equity/Bond

From a return on shareholders' equity standpoint, we can argue that if Freddie Mac can maintain the average annual return on shareholders' equity that it earned over the last six years, 22.3%, and that over the next ten years it annually retains approximately 72% of that return (approximately the average percentage that it retained over the last six years), then per share equity value should grow from $4.92 a share in 1992 to approximately $21.79 a share by the year 2002.

If per share equity value is $21.79 in 2002 and Freddie Mac is still earning a 22.3% return on shareholders' equity, then Freddie Mac should report per share earnings of $4.86 a share ($21.79 × .223 = $4.86). If Freddie Mac is trading at its historical low P/E of 9, this will equate to a market price of $43.74 a share. Multiplied by the historical high P/E of 12.8, you get a per share market price of $62.20. Add in an estimated dividend pay out of approximately $7.61 a share and you get a total pretax return of somewhere between $51.35 and $69.81. (You can get these figures by taking out the TI calculator and punching in $9.67 for the present value (PV), 10 for the number of years (N); and either $51.35 or $69.81 for the future value (FV). Hit the CPT key followed by i% key, and you get either 18.17% or 21.85%.)

This means that Warren's investment of $9.67 a share in 1992 is projected to produce a pretax annual compounding rate of return of between 18.17% and 21.85%. (When adjusted for corporate income taxes this equates to an annual compounding after-tax rate of return of between 14.82% and 17.92% for the ten years between 1992 and 2002. ($100,000 compounding at an annual rate of 17.92% would be worth $519,845 in ten years' time).

### Projecting an Annual Compounding Rate of Return Using the Historical Annual per Share Earnings Growth Figure

Warren can figure that if per share earnings continue to grow at a rate of 17.6% annually, and if Freddie Mac continues to pay out dividends at a rate of 28% of per share earnings, then the following per share earnings and dividend disbursement picture will develop over the next ten years:

| Year | Projected Earnings | Projected Dividends |
|------|--------------------|---------------------|
| 1993 | $0.96 | $0.27 |
| 1994 | $1.13 | $0.31 |
| 1995 | $1.33 | $0.37 |
| 1996 | $1.56 | $0.43 |
| 1997 | $1.84 | $0.51 |
| 1998 | $2.16 | $0.60 |
| 1999 | $2.55 | $0.71 |
| 2000 | $2.99 | $0.83 |
| 2001 | $3.52 | $0.98 |
| 2002 | $4.14 | $1.16 |
|      |       | $6.17 |

This means that in 2002 Warren can project that Freddie Mac will have per share earnings of $4.14. If Freddie Mac is trading at its lowest price to earnings ratio since it started actively being traded—9—then we can calculate that market price for the stock in 2002 will be $37.26 ($4.14 × 9 = $37.26).

If it is trading at its highest P/E—12.8—then we can calculate that market price for the stock will be $52.99 in 2004.

If you spent $9.67 for a share of Freddie Mac stock in 1992 and in ten years it was worth somewhere between $37.26 and $52.99 a share, then your pretax annual compounding rate of return will be somewhere between 14.4% and 18.5%. (You can get these figures by taking out the TI calculator and punching in $9.67 for the present value (PV); 10 for the number of years (N); and either $37.26 or $52.99 for the future value (FV). Hit the CPT key followed by i% and your rate of return will appear.)

If we add in the dividends, which total $6.17, our projected pretax return jumps to somewhere between $43.43 and $59.16, which equates to a pretax annual compounding rate of return between 16.2% and 19.8%.

## In Summary

In 1992 Warren bought approximately 34,844,400 shares of Freddie Mac common stock at approximately $9.67 a share, for a total purchase price of $337 million. When Warren bought the stock he could argue that he had just bought a Freddie Mac equity/bond with an initial rate of return of 8.5% that would grow at a rate of approximately 17.6% a year. He could also figure that if he held the stock for 10 years, his pretax annual compounding rate of return would be between 16.2% and 21.85%.

## How Accurate Were Our Freddie Mac Projections?

Just how accurate were our projections? Let's take a look and see:

| Year | Projected Earnings | Actual Earnings | Margin of Error |
|---|---|---|---|
| 1993 | $.96 | $1.02 | +1.1% |
| 1994 | $1.13 | $1.27 | +12.3% |
| 1995 | $1.33 | $1.42 | +6.7% |
| 1996 | $1.56 | $1.65 | +5.7% |
| 1997 | $1.84 | $1.90 | +3.2% |
| 1998 | $2.16 | $2.13 | −1.3% |
| 1999 | $2.55 | $2.96 | +16% |

Remember, we are making long-term earnings projections, which is unheard of on Wall Street. From the looks of things, our projections seemed a tad conservative with Freddie Mac turning in a better-than-expected performance in six out of the last seven years. Not bad. In 1999 the stock traded in the range of $45.40 to $65.30 a share. If Warren had sold his stock in 1999, which he bought for $9.67 a share in 1992, his pretax annual compounding rate of return, excluding dividends, would have been somewhere between 24.7% and 31.3%, or approximately eight to ten percentage points above our projections. Like we said, companies that have consumer monopolies, like Freddie Mac, have economic engines that bring investors more happy surprises than unhappy ones. That is why Warren keeps getting richer.

## CASE STUDY THREE: MCDONALD'S CORPORATION, 1996

Warren has long been fascinated with fast food, and he is particularly interested in restaurant chains like McDonald's, which has taken a generic food like the hamburger and turned it into a brand name product. During 1996 Berkshire Hathaway purchased 60,313,200 shares of McDonald's at an average cost of $20.97 a share. Let's see why Warren found McDonald's so attractive. (Please note that the historical figures presented in the McDonald's case study reflect a two-for-one split that occurred in 1999).

### Doing Your Detective Work

The way the product works is easy. You eat it.

Go to the library. Check out *Value Line,* find the listing for McDonald's Corp., photocopy it, then go to the *Guide to Business Periodicals* and pull out a list of magazine articles on the company. Either call the company (630-623-7428) and ask for an annual report or go on-line and checkout McDonald's Web site at www.mcdonalds.com to retrieve updated financial information about the company. After you have assembled all your information, read on. (Remember, that is how you did things a mere four years ago. Now you can just drop onto the Internet, go to the McDonald's Web site, and pull up a plethora of financial information.)

1. Does the company have an IDENTIFIABLE CONSUMER MONOPOLY OR BRAND NAME PRODUCTS or does it produce a commodity type of product? Have you ever eaten a McDonald's hamburger? You would be hard pressed to find anybody who hasn't. McDonald's is the world's largest restaurant chain. With more than 20,000 restaurants in 100 plus countries around the world, it's hard to put any real distance between you and Ronald McDonald. In fact, McDonald's has sold more hamburgers than there are people in the world. Quite a feat.

Yes, McDonald's has an identifiable consumer monopoly brand name product.

2. Is the company CONSERVATIVELY FINANCED? The company has long-term debts that account for 35% of its capital structure, which is conservative, given its long history of strong earnings.

3. Are the EARNINGS of the company strong and do they show an upward trend? A check of the company's earnings indicates that they have been growing at a rate of 13.5% compounded annually for the period from 1986 to 1996, and at a rate of 13.26% for the last five years. Earnings can be considered very consistent, increasing every year for the last ten years.

A fast look at the yearly per share earnings—

| Year | Earnings |
|------|----------|
| 1986 | $0.31 |
| 1987 | $0.36 |
| 1988 | $0.43 |
| 1989 | $0.49 |
| 1990 | $0.55 |
| 1991 | $0.59 |
| 1992 | $0.65 |
| 1993 | $0.73 |
| 1994 | $0.84 |
| 1995 | $0.99 |
| 1996 | $1.11 |

—indicates they are strong and have an upward trend, which is what we are looking for.

4. The company allocates capital only to those businesses within its REALM OF EXPERTISE, which in this case means expansion of its operations.

5. Further investigation indicates that the company has been buying back its shares.

6. The manner in which management has spent the retained earnings of the company appears to have increased the per share earnings and therefore SHAREHOLDER VALUE.

From 1986 to 1996 the company had retained earnings of $5.74 a share. Per share earnings grew by $0.80 a share, from $0.31 at the end of 1986 to $1.11 by the end of 1996. Thus, we can argue that the retained earnings of $5.74 a share produced in 1996 an after–corporate income tax return of $.80 a share, which equates to a rate of return of 13.9%. This indicates that there has been a profitable allocation of retained earnings and a corresponding increase in per share earnings. This has caused a parallel increase in the market price for the company's stock from approximately $5.00 a share in 1986 to approximately $23.50 in 1996.

7. The company's RETURN ON SHAREHOLDERS' EQUITY IS ABOVE AVERAGE. As we know, Warren considers it a good sign when a business can earn above average returns on shareholders' equity. The average return on shareholders' equity for American corporations over the last thirty years is approximately 12%. The return on shareholders' equity for the McDonald's Corporation in the ten years between 1986 and 1996 looked like this—

| Year | R.O.E. |
|------|--------|
| 1986 | 19.1% |
| 1987 | 18.8% |
| 1988 | 18.9% |
| 1989 | 20.5% |
| 1990 | 19.2% |
| 1991 | 17.8% |
| 1992 | 16.0% |
| 1993 | 17.3% |
| 1994 | 17.8% |
| 1995 | 18.2% |
| 1996 | 18.0% |

—which gives you an average annual rate of return on shareholders' equity for the last ten years of 18.25%. More important than averages is the fact that the company has earned consistently high returns on shareholders' equity. This indicates that McDonald's management does an excellent job of profitably allocating retained earnings.

8. IS THE COMPANY FREE TO ADJUST PRICES TO INFLATION? This is an easy one, because we all remember paying 15¢

for a McDonald's hamburger, which now costs approximated $1.20. So we answer this question with a *yes*. Inflation will not affect the demand for McDonald's products, nor will it stop McDonald's from passing any increase in production costs on to the consumer.

9. McDONALD'S OPERATIONS DO NOT REQUIRE LARGE CAPITAL EXPENDITURES TO CONSTANTLY UPDATE THE COMPANY'S PLANT AND EQUIPMENT. There really isn't any research and development going on here and the franchisees are responsible for the costs of building most of the restaurants.

### Summary of Data

Since Warren gets positive responses to the above key questions, he concludes that this is a company that he can fit into his "realm of confidence" and that its earnings can be predicted with a fair degree of certainty.

## PRICE ANALYSIS INITIAL RATE OF RETURN AND RELATIVE VALUE TO GOVERNMENT BONDS

McDonald's had per share earnings in 1996 of $1.11 a share. Divide $1.11 by the interest rate on long-term government bonds in 1996, approximately 7%, and you get a relative value of $15.85 share ($1.11 ÷ 0.07 = $15.85).

During 1996 you could have bought a share of McDonald's stock for as little as $20.50 a share and as much as $27. Since 1996 per share earnings were $1.11 a share, if you had paid between $20.50 and $27, your initial rate of return would be between 4.1% and 5.4%. Warren's average cost was $20.97, which equates to an initial rate of return of 5.29%.

A review of McDonald's per share earnings growth rate for the last ten years indicates that the company has been growing at an annual compounding rate of 13.6%. So if you were Warren, you could have asked yourself this question: Which would I rather own—a government bond with a static rate of return of 7% or a McDonald's equity/bond with an initial rate of return of 5.29% that is increasing at an annual rate of 13.6%?

### McDonald's Stock as an Equity/Bond

From a return on shareholders' equity standpoint, we can argue that in 1996 McDonald's had a per share equity value of $6.02. If McDonald's can maintain its ten-year average rate of return on shareholders' equity of 18.25% and retain approximately 84% of that return, with 16% being paid out as a dividend, then McDonald's per share equity value should grow at an annual compounding rate of 15.33% year (84% of 18.25% is 15.33%). If McDonald's per share equity value grows at a rate of 15.33% a year, it will reach approximately $25.06 a share by Year 10, 2006.

If per share equity value is $25.06 in Year 10 and McDonald's is still earning an 18.25% return on shareholders' equity, then McDonald's should report per share earnings of $4.57 ($25.06 × .1825 = $4.57). If McDonald's is trading at its average ten-year price to earnings ratio, a P/E of 16.7, then we can project that the market price for a share of McDonald's stock in 2006 will be $76.31 ($4.57 × 16.7 = $76.31). Add in the dividend pool of approximately $3.75 a share and our total proceeds jump to $80.06 a share. Total proceeds of $80.06 a share equate to a pretax annual compounding rate of return of approximately 14.3%.

This means that if you, like Warren, had paid $20.97 a share in 1996 and sold your investment in 2006, you could expect a pretax annual compounding rate of return of 14.3%.

## Projecting an Annual Compounding Rate of Return Using the Historical Annual per Share Earnings Growth Figure

Warren can figure that if per share earnings for McDonald's were $1.11 in 1996, and they continue to grow at a rate of 13.6% annually and it continues to pay out dividends at a rate of 16% of per share earnings, then the following per share earnings and dividend disbursement picture will develop over the next ten years:

| Year | Earnings | Dividends |
|------|----------|-----------|
| 1997 | $1.26 | $0.20 |
| 1998 | $1.43 | $0.22 |
| 1999 | $1.62 | $0.26 |
| 2000 | $1.84 | $0.29 |
| 2001 | $2.09 | $0.33 |
| 2002 | $2.38 | $0.38 |
| 2003 | $2.71 | $0.43 |
| 2004 | $3.07 | $0.49 |
| 2005 | $3.49 | $0.55 |
| 2006 | $3.97 | $0.63 |
| | | $3.78 |

This means that in 2006 we can project that McDonald's will have per share earnings of $3.97 a share. If McDonald's is trading at its average ten-year price to earnings ratio, a P/E of 16.7, then we can calculate that the market price for a share of McDonald's stock in 2006 will be $66.29 ($3.97 × 16.7 = $66.29).

If you, like Warren, had spent $20.97 for a share of McDonald's stock in 1996 and in ten years it is worth approximately $66.29 a share, then your pretax annual compounding rate of return would be approximately 12.19%. (You can get these figures on the TI calculator by punching in $20.97 for the present value (PV), 10 for the number of years (N), and $66.29 for the future value (FV). Hit the CPT key followed by i% and your pretax annual compounding rate of return will appear—12.19%).

If we add in the dividends that McDonald's will have paid out, a total of $3.78, to the $66.29 projected 2006 share price, then our total proceeds from the sale increase to $70.07 a share, which gives us a projected pretax annual compounding rate of return of 12.8%.

## In Summary

In 1996 Warren bought 60,313,200 shares of McDonald's Corporation common stock at an average price of $20.97 a share, for a total purchase price of approximately $1.265 billion. When he bought the stock he could argue that he had just bought a McDonald's equity/bond with an initial rate of return of 5.29% that would grow at a rate of approximately 13.6% a year. He could also figure that if he held the stock for ten years, his pretax annual compounding rate of return would be between 12.8% and 14.3%.

## How Accurate Were Warren's McDonald's Projections?

How accurate were Warren's projections? In this case we have actual figures up through 1999 to check against his projections. So let's take a look and see just how well Warren has done.

### PROJECTED EARNINGS COMPARED TO ACTUAL EARNINGS

| Year | Projected Earnings | Actual Earnings | Margin of Error |
|------|--------------------|-----------------|-----------------|
| 1997 | $1.26 | $1.15 | −8.7% |
| 1998 | $1.43 | $1.26 | −11.8% |
| 1999 | $1.62 | $1.41 | −12.9% |

As you can see, our projections were off by an average of 11.1%. It's not an exact science. In 1999 McDonald's stock traded in a range from $35.90 to $49.60 a share. On Warren's original investment of $20.97 a share, made in 1996, a selling price of $35.90 a share in 1999 would have resulted in a pretax annual compounding rate of return, excluding dividends, of 19.6%. If he had sold it for $49.60 a share his annual compounding rate of return, excluding dividends, would have been 33.2%, which is a far more interesting number to take to the bank.

## A FINAL WORD

One more word of advice: Warren once said that the hardest thing in the world to do is be patient. So don't be in a hurry! You will find a consumer monopoly selling at the right price, and it will offer you the opportunity to make a fortune. You might not find the perfect situation overnight, but occasionally the bad news situation and the stock market's short-sightedness serves them up to us on a platter of gold. You only have to reach out and pick one up. It's that easy.